A WAY TO HAPPINESS

A WAY TO HAPPINESS

With White Eagle as Guide in Meditation

YLANA HAYWARD

THE WHITE EAGLE PUBLISHING TRUST

NEW LANDS · LISS · HAMPSHIRE · ENGLAND

First published 1995

© *Copyright, Ylana Hayward and*
The White Eagle Publishing Trust, 1995

British Library
Cataloguing-in-Publication Data

A catalogue record for this book is
available from the British Library

ISBN 0-85487-094-6

Set in 12.5 on 14.5pt Monotype Spectrum by
the publisher and printed and bound in Great Britain
at the University Press, Cambridge

CONTENTS

ILLUSTRATIONS

The White Eagle Publishing Trust is part of the wider work of the White Eagle Lodge, a meeting place or fraternity in which people may find a place for growth and understanding, and a place in which the teachings of White Eagle find practical expression. Here men and women may come to learn the reason for their life on earth and how to serve and live in harmony with the whole brotherhood of life, visible and invisible, in health and happiness.

Readers wishing to know more of the work of the White Eagle Lodge may write to the General Secretary, The White Eagle Lodge, New Lands, Brewells Lane, Liss, Hampshire, England GU33 7HY (tel. 01730 893300) or can call at The White Eagle Lodge, 9 St Mary Abbots Place, Kensington, London W8 6LS (tel. 0171-603 7914). In the Americas please write to Church of the White Eagle Lodge, P. O. Box 930, Montgomery, Texas 77356 (tel. 409-597 5757), and in Australasia to The White Eagle Lodge (Australasia), Willomee, P. O. Box 225, Maleny, Queensland 4552 (tel. 074 944397). A variety of activities is held at all these addresses.

INTRODUCTION
by Colum Hayward

It has been suggested that I write a few words of introduction to this book written by my mother, Ylana Hayward, and I feel I should like to begin with a little story that demonstrates the power of meditation.

One autumn day not so long ago I found myself developing a feverish cold. I had been through a time when my energies were stretched out in all directions through overwork; conventionally, it was hardly surprising to catch a cold. The symptoms were severe enough for me to lie on my bed, hoping they'd go away. Outside, I could see blue sky broken by white clouds, and the leaves of a London plane tree shaking in the wind. It was good just to relax.

Slowly, I got caught up in the gentle rhythms of movement of the leaves, and the great sweep of the clouds across the vastness of sky. I wasn't in direct sunlight, but I could see it in patches of brightness on the leaves, and bright edges to the clouds.

On and on, the movement went. Although I made no conscious effort to do so, I became nonetheless completely absorbed in the dance of nature I was watching. Somehow, it put me much more in touch with myself than I had been for weeks. I felt part of the natural world, part of the universe, part of God.

Slowly, I drifted off to sleep; and when I awoke, the fever had left me.

This is not a remarkable story; it is simply a reminder that has stayed with me of the power that lies in simple contact with one's Self. My fever was slight, and went easily. But the story shows how naturally disposed we all are to meditate in a simple way, and also the power that meditation has to centre the self and enable us to reconnect with the universe.

Although in this book there is much instruction about how to use meditation in the fullest way, and a great deal of help with the actual technique of meditation, I do not think there is a better start for the beginner than to remember the times when we actually *are* meditating, even without realizing it. When we go for a walk and get caught up simply in the enjoyment of it, with no distracting worries going on in our heads, when we absorb the sunshine and attune ourselves to the natural rhythm of life, as I did, that time; when we sit quietly, unpreoccupied, perhaps listening to our breathing, we are beginning to meditate. Meditation is then precisely what it always will be, even when our technique is more developed:

the time when we are not distracted away from our self-awareness. It is an absolutely natural time in which the self is heard; and through that contact with the true self, the voice of God is heard also.

Here is something White Eagle once said; I think it draws us on rather beautifully from the idea of simply listening, watching, as meditation, and shows us the enormous potential that there is when we listen, in the deep sense of the word.

If you could but give yourselves time to withdraw from the outer or material planes of life, and *listen!* When sitting at peace in your garden, or walking in the open places within your towns, or in quiet country lanes, give yourselves time to listen to the voice of love, which will then surely make itself known in the quiet of your soul.

This, beloved brethren, is the great secret of life on the earth plane. Those who live on the material plane only are barren, are starved; whatever work they put their hand to do, if they are not contacting the spirit, or the voice of God, in the quiet of their own souls, they do not dwell in the fullness they were intended to by our Father. He has given unto His children the gift of love, the gift of wisdom, which lies in the heart. Another name for this gift is the spirit of Christ.

Test our words for yourselves; observe those

who are trying, according to their own under-standing, to express artistic, musical or literary gifts, or the gift of healing, and note how many of these are in touch with that mysterious spiritual life. Those so in touch express the life of the spirit in their work; others working purely on the intel-lectual plane may give brilliant service, brilliant work to the world, but there is something lacking if the spirit does not shine through. In a perfectly executed piece of music—technically perfect—unless the spirit is within, it fails in its purpose. So cultivate the art of listening, in your quiet mo-ments, to the spirit, and it will speak ever in one language, that of love. Love brings to your heart peace, kindliness, tolerance, a desire to forget selfish aims, and a longing to give that which your spirit has revealed to you, to the rest of humanity.

from THE WAY OF THE SUN, pp. 39–40

*

The present book is subtitled 'With White Eagle as Guide in Meditation' and the phrase perhaps needs a little explanation for those who do not know White Eagle as a teacher. First, I hope that the passage just quoted gives an indication of the beauty of his teach-ing, and the clear sense of it coming not from the ordinary human consciousness—what White Eagle would call the frontal mind—but from a source in great harmony with the real source of life. White Eagle is a spirit guide, and he has been speaking, addressing himself not only to people's everyday consciousness but to what he would call the 'higher mind', for many years now. While his teaching makes perfect sense to the everyday mind, it makes far more sense when the everyday mind is not too busy and the love behind the words can more easily be heard: that is to say, when precisely the consciousness that we allow in meditation is starting to operate. For those who find it difficult to accept that words can come 'from spirit', through an earthly medium, I would like to say, 'don't worry'. If it feels to you that the words are coming from the medium's own consciousness, perhaps operating at a higher level, then all it demonstrates is the tremendous power that the higher consciousness of every one of us can hold! If it feels more than this to you, so much the better. But if, on the other hand, the words do not strike you with particular power, if they do not touch your heart, then probably White Eagle is not the teacher for you right now. We hope you will nonetheless enjoy whatever sort of meditation you choose to follow.

A WAY TO HAPPINESS is a book both for beginners, and for people who have been meditating long enough to have their own crop of questions to ask. It was born out of my mother's long experience as a teacher of meditation, itself a training passed on to her by her mother, White Eagle's medium Grace Cooke. It is also deeply influenced, as the title implies, by her very profound acquaintance with White Eagle as teacher; there is no-one better fitted than she to write about the whole way of life based on meditation which has been lived in the Lodge for nearly sixty years. And it is this *way of life*, which is so much more than the isolated practice of a morning meditation, that is special about the White Eagle way.

Meditation teaching began in the Lodge very soon after it was founded in 1936. At that time, the practice of meditation was quite unusual in the West (despite perfectly good roots for its practice in the Christian monastic tradition, principally through the example of the fourth-century Desert Fathers in Egypt). Grace Cooke's own introduction to meditation came as a surprise even to herself, and perhaps it will be of interest to readers to recount it here. An Indian visitor was invited to the Lodge in London by a mutual friend, though he arrived quite unannounced. He meditated in the chapel for some time, and came back a couple of days later with a fellow Hindu as a companion. Let Minesta (as Grace Cooke was so widely known among her friends) take up the story herself:

On this occasion he asked for me and suggested that I should meditate with them. This period of meditation proved to be another experience of spiritual illumination. Not through my own strength, but through the help of these two unknown brothers, I was so raised in consciousness and freed from the limitation of my mortal self, that I became increasingly aware of a state of heavenly bliss in which I was conscious of spiritual illumination and indeed ecstasy, as well as the power of creative life-forces. In this state of cosmic consciousness I knew (but only for a fleeting moment) the eternal presence of the infinite Father. I knew also of the maternal aspect of God—the eternal Mother—in fact the predominating Presence at our meditation was that of the great Mother. Although this experience lasted only a few minutes, the revelation it brought has remained in my memory as fresh and living as when it first came.

from THE SHINING PRESENCE, p. 27

Of her books, it is probably MEDITATION that will be of most interest to readers, for it has long been a classic in its field and is in no way superseded by the present volume. Minesta followed it with the book THE JEWEL IN THE LOTUS, which is unique in its interpretation of the symbols that come to students—here her own students—in meditation.

Minesta used to lead a regular spiritual unfoldment class in the Lodge, often giving way as teacher to White Eagle himself. As an outcome of these classes a set of four short books was brought out in the 1940s, called, appropriately, SPIRITUAL UNFOLDMENT, each of them containing White Eagle's teaching. There is a current series too, offering a different selection of teaching. Anyone who reads the first volume of this second series will see how meditation can be a path as well as a practice; though in the phrase 'the practice of the presence of God', path and practice perhaps come together, which is White Eagle's ideal.

Minesta's life focused above all upon the task of helping people overcome the fear of death. White Eagle's teaching deeply reinforces people's knowledge and awareness of the wonderful consciousness that continues after physical death. In respect of this, White Eagle would say that meditation offers better reassurance than psychic contact; he predicted that in the future men and women would not seek those they loved in the world of light through another person, but that each would be his or her own medium, building the bridge between the two worlds through meditation and inner awareness. People would find all the strength and guidance and comfort they needed, both in bereavement and in the general demands that life makes, by learning how to 'tune in' to the source of life in their own being; by consciously discovering the God within themselves.

Perhaps this view of the significance of meditation is one reason why, in the White Eagle way, it is indeed a complete way of life, not just a technique. It also explains why meditation teaching in the Lodge also centres on the retreats which are held at New Lands, country headquarters of the Lodge in Hampshire, England (and, nowadays, also at the Lodge's centres in the Americas and Australasia and elsewhere). These retreats provide an opportunity to be at one with nature, at the same time as to harmonize with a group of like-minded people. Meditating in a group is a feature of the White Eagle way; while there is absolutely nothing 'missing' in meditating on your own, the group is a reminder that we simply are not alone, ever; in meditation we shed some of the coats of individuality and reach upwards to a level where a much closer communion with all, as well as with the Source, is possible. A regular group meditation is held at the Lodge, and there are classes which lead up to this, providing training.

The group meditations and the training have led, over the years, to a regular feature on meditation in the White Eagle magazine *Stella Polaris* (the name means simply the Pole Star or guiding star), and it is from these articles that much of the book derives. Chapters five and six are based entirely on questions that have been put to my mother as editor of *Stella*

Polaris. She and her sister Joan Hodgson write a regular column in the magazine and in the present book the reader may find the pronoun 'we' is a nice reminder of the way in which they have together taken on the mantle of principal teacher of the White Eagle way of meditation after Minesta's passing in 1979. The seventh chapter, 'Tree of Light', also arises from *Stella Polaris*; my mother devised this simple breathing routine herself and published it in an article in 1980; over the years, she has revised and expanded it for her own practice and the result is the much fuller version given in this book.

Chapter eight begins what is properly a second section, namely teachings by White Eagle himself, given to groups of students, each one of them touching on meditation in one way or another. These teachings take the student further into what may be discovered in meditation: into the mysteries, as it were. Except for 'The Divine Magic', which appears under a different title in SPIRITUAL UNFOLDMENT 3, these teachings have not previously been published in book form, and where quotations from White Eagle have not been ascribed, they too are from teaching as yet unpublished in book form.

CHAPTER I

When the soul seeks illumination

FOR MORE than half a century now, the teacher whom we have come to know and love as White Eagle, the messenger, has been leading us through meditation to find the place, deep in the stillness and silence of the heart, where love dwells—love, the Christ-spirit—and in so doing to find the strength and wisdom and guidance for life's journey.

To our brethren from the East, this centre of peace and stillness deep within is seen as a lotus flower of perfect purity, wherein is cradled the shining jewel which we call the Christ-spirit. For most, that little light, that Christ light, is hidden, covered over with layers of materialistic thought or 'earthiness'; using again the symbolism of the East, the petals of the lotus flower are closed, and the jewel within is hidden. But there comes a time when the soul longs for illumination; longs, consciously or unconsciously, for God. It is reaching out to the source from which it came. It wants knowledge, and understanding of life's mysteries; it longs to know whence it came and whither it is bound; or perhaps it just longs to serve and to give and to love, or to express itself in worship and thankfulness.

With that aspiration, the petals of the lotus begin to open and reveal the shining jewel of the Christ-spirit. Through aspiration and meditation, that beautiful flower, which for so many is a closed bud, gradually opens to the sunlight from above, to the sunlight of the Great Spirit, and the jewel within is revealed in all its beauty. It grows in size and radiance to illumine the whole life and to heal and to bless and bring light to others.

That jewel, that light in the heart, is from the Sun, from the heart of the Great Spirit. White Eagle says:

From the Sun we all come, to the Sun we all return....

God said, 'Let there be light,' and there was light; and from that light everything was created. From that light we have come; to that light we return, ourselves beings of light, rich in experience, having gained wisdom, love and power, having grown at the end of that journey to the full stature of the son—daughter of God, complete, perfect.

from THE STILL VOICE, pp. 111-112

It is to this journey home to the Sun that we are

led in meditation: a return to the full consciousness of the Sun life from which we came; to total heart-realization of our union with God, and the oneness of all life. If this sounds too remote from everyday life, too hard to attain, let us put it more simply. Through meditation we are led to find strength, wisdom, and guidance for life's journey and the answer to every need. Through meditation we can find true and lasting happiness. Through meditation also, and this needs always to be part of our motive, we learn to become better servants of the light, better channels for the light from the Great Spirit, and thus better able to heal and to help where help is needed.

There are many different schools of meditation, many different approaches to the meditative state. Some may follow one path, some another, but all paths should lead, in the end, to the same goal—the realization of God in the heart, and union with God, the heart of God, in the Sun. Nevertheless, it is important, when we have found what we feel to be the right path for us, to remain true to it and not waste energy and perhaps become confused by trying to follow several ways at the same time.

There are also many degrees of the meditative state, of withdrawal from the outer world to inner quietness. A certain level of quiet withdrawal can be found simply through prayer; some can find it through the uplifting power of music. Some will touch this inner stillness and joyful illumination through contact with nature—perhaps standing with their back against a tall tree and sharing its life; or alone on the English Downs under a wide sky, with a lark singing; or perhaps high among mountains, or beholding the beauty of a flower and inhaling its perfume. All these experiences can touch something deep in the heart and help to awaken the light that is shining there. But none of these is really quite the same as that state of consciousness reached through the discipline of meditation—and it certainly is a discipline, though a very rewarding one.

Even then, there are levels and levels of meditation—from the five or ten minutes' quiet time before the start of the day to that deep and prolonged withdrawal we can make, away from the outer mind and towards the timeless centre within, when consciousness of the world of matter recedes utterly and the soul rests in oneness with the Infinite.

White Eagle's method is clear and safe and does not demand great intellectual effort, for he guides us to work purely from the heart, and to use what he calls the 'heart-mind'. The heart-mind is not centred in the head as is the little mind of every day, or as is the proud intellect, but it is consciousness centred in the heart. It is nonetheless a marriage of the heart and the head. It is the higher, creative mind, the mind which all creators of beauty in form consciously or unconsciously use.

Our first aim, when entering into meditation, must always be to quieten the outer mind; to empty it of all extraneous thought. It is not easy, particularly in the noisy mental confusion of our western world, totally to make the mind blank, empty; certainly not in the early stages of meditation, before we have learnt how to go to that stillness which lies beneath all thought. That is why, in creative meditation, White Eagle teaches us to use that higher mind to create an image of beauty upon which we can focus our awareness, so that the mind is so absorbed in this image of beauty that there is no space left for all the worrying little thoughts of everyday life. Then, as will be explained later, from this first image the consciousness gradually expands into an inner timeless world, where we can learn to hear truth beyond words, or be taught by the guide of our spirit, according to our need; and above all, we are led to find that deep inner centre where all is love.

One of the most helpful images upon which to concentrate initially is that of a still flame. To hold the image of the flame clear and pure there must be no whisper of earthly thought to disturb its stillness. Indeed, whenever you meditate it is helpful to sit in a prepared place, with a candle or a little light burning before you. It can be quite simple. Just a comfortable chair, set before a small table on which the candle or little lamp burns, will do; or better still, set aside a corner in your home which you always use for your meditation. This applies whether you are alone or meet with a small group of friends (a good thing to do, for in working together in this way you all help each other). You will find that a quietness will gather in the place you set aside, a peace which will help you in your withdrawal from the everyday world.

It is helpful also to set aside the same hour each day for your meditation, whether it be a brief time of quiet attunement, or a longer, deeper period of withdrawal. For most people, first thing in the morning is the easiest time, and also the most helpful, because the true 'heart-contact' that you make then can carry you through your day. But whatever time you choose, try, if possible, to keep to it each day. The regular rhythm, though not essential, is helpful; at the same time, don't feel bound or burdened by it. Let your meditation be a real joy and something to which you look forward, whether it is just a brief time at the start of the day and no more or a longer period of deep meditation when time is of no consequence.

CHAPTER II

Using the posture

ONE OF the lessons we are learning on the spiritual path is how to touch the heights of spiritual awareness without losing our grip on practical matters. *Head in heaven, feet firmly on earth,* is the rule.

This is true of meditation too, in the sense that in meditation we need at all times to remain in complete control of the body, and yet be unaffected by any bodily sensation. A yogi can go so deeply into meditation that he is totally unmoved by anything outside his body, because he is so much in control of it. Few of us have reached that stage yet, though it is perfectly possible, even for us as students, to be so intensely in the inner world as to be largely unaffected by the pull of the body, or any sounds from the outside world.

One of the ways in which the yogi attains this state of complete control and yet detachment is to adopt a certain meditative posture—for instance the lotus posture—in which the body is perfectly poised and balanced and closed within itself. Not many of us will feel we can even attempt this; nevertheless, to attain the true and deep meditative state, bodily poise and discipline are essential—discipline which extends to the mind and emotional system as well, for each affects the other. Poise of body leads to poise of mind, and vice versa.

It is important, in the first place, that the body should be as comfortable as possible. When you sit for meditation it is worth taking some initial trouble to ensure that the chair you choose is the right height for you, and that the back of the chair is at the correct angle, so that you can sit naturally upright without effort. (See the picture on p. 27. It is much better not to use the back as a rest if possible, but if you do need this support, make sure that it holds you directly upright: polarized, as it were, between heaven and earth.) This upright, balanced posture imparts a wonderful feeling of inner strength and stillness, a sense of control from within—as if you, the shining spirit, are master in the temple of your body.

All muscular tension can now be relaxed. Much tension centres in the shoulders and at the back of the neck, so try shrugging your shoulders once or twice, gently, and then letting your shoulders drop, and your arms hang loosely by your side for a minute or two. Above all, relax your facial muscles, and those of the brow particularly—no screwed-up forehead, trying so hard to concentrate! Just let go. You are relaxing at what the eastern system of the chakras calls the brow centre (see below, p. 33).

You are now consciously relaxed, yet still perfectly balanced and upright and ready to assume the position recommended by my mother Grace Cooke in her book MEDITATION—that is, the right ankle laid across the left, and the left hand lying loosely cupped in the right. Let your feeling as you do this be one of inner surrender and a quiet waiting upon God, poised yet relaxed.

You may be asking: 'Why do we adopt this posture of ankles crossed and hands cupped one within the other? This seals in the energies of one's body; would it not also close one off from spiritual influence?'

The reason we adopt this posture for meditation has more to do with the magnetic or energy patterns of the body than with 'spiritual influences', as they might be described. White Eagle tells us that we give with the right hand and receive with the left; so if the hands are cupped and the ankles are crossed, the circle is complete, and we are within a cocoon of energy of our own creating. This circle helps to protect us from intrusion from the lower astral level of life: that is, life at the lower levels of consciousness, which can pull us down and away from our true path.

Remember that the world in which you become aware in meditation is an inner or soul world; you are not going out into any condition outside yourself, you are going within. But at the same time, by one of those contradictions which abound on the spiritual path, your consciousness is expanding, you are rising into the heart of the Sun, and you are doing this from within. Our ability to receive from the spirit is not in any way affected by this wrapping of ourselves in a cocoon of light and energy. In fact, we could say that the sealing and shutting down at that astral level of what White Eagle calls the etheric body—that is, the invisible or soul body—helps the aspirant in meditation to be more aware of, and more responsive to, the true guidance and influence from the higher planes of life. It can be seen as a way of preparing to receive. As we close down at the lower level we are enabled to make a direct, clear contact with the true world of spirit.

What is beautiful about the hand posture described is the way in which you present a cup, waiting to be filled with divine light. If you find that actually cupping your hands together and crossing your ankles makes you uncomfortable, it may be that just keeping the feeling of forming that cup, but actually allowing your hands to be slightly apart, perhaps even

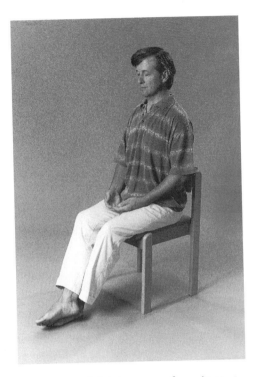

A recommended sitting posture for meditation

palm upwards one on each knee, is a better way to meditate for you. In the picture above you will see this quite flexible approach, and also get a good sense of the back held upright but not stiffly so. With re- gard to the ankles, the crossed position is best (as shown in the picture); but to have the feet flat on the floor, if you find this more comfortable, gives you a good 'grounding', and this may itself be useful if, for instance, you have a tendency to 'float' in an uncontrolled way in the meditation.

Each small act that is part of the ritual of entering into meditation—the bodily posture, the position of hands and feet, the deliberate relaxing of muscular tension—is important, but none is more important than the correct breathing. In White Eagle's meditation we have a very simple method which everyone can use without strain or pitfall.

When you are preparing for meditation, having made sure that you are sitting comfortably—relaxed and yet poised and alert, as described earlier—let your next thought always and without fail be for your breathing. It is quite helpful to start by giving a big sigh, and as you let the air out, let your head fall gently forward and your shoulders hang loosely. Feel that all the cares of the world are dropping from your shoulders. Then gently straighten, sit poised and erect again and start simply to listen to your breathing. Feel that you are observing it in the same way as you might watch the movement of the sea.

Doing this, before long you should find that you are breathing more slowly and deeply. To deepen the breath does not mean to imply the strain and discomfort of filling the lungs to bursting-point. We are talking of a movement which is not only slow, but gentle and infinitely relaxing. The word 'deeply' refers to the part of the lungs being filled, rather than to the volume of the breath. As you breathe, feel that the lower rib-cage is gently expanding on the inbreathing and returning to the relaxed position on the outbreathing. You might like to try this independently of meditation for a little while, until it becomes almost automatic. When you feel that you have mastered this simple movement, then it is time to apply it to your meditation, or indeed at any time of the day when you want to turn within to the centre of quietness and stillness in your heart. For your meditation it is quite helpful to establish a rhythmic pattern with the breathing, and this is something unique to each of us; you may like to work on a series of six or seven breaths, or perhaps even just three.

Suppose you start by taking six slow, deep 'lower rib-cage' breaths and while doing this concentrate wholly on the physical movement—the gently moving rib-cage, the beautifully relaxed feeling of your shoulders and arms hanging loose and relaxed by your side (it is interesting that this sensation seems to spread to the area of the throat centre too). Listen deeply to the quiet sound of your own breathing. Now you may begin to get a feeling of withdrawing from the outer world; already the mind is becoming stiller, for there is no room in it for wayward thought.

Your whole being is centred within. Now, quietly start on a new cycle of breaths and with them try to become aware of the quiet rhythms of nature, as though you were breathing with them, breathing with the earth as she breathes, with the tides, the seasons as they come and go—all the rhythms of eternity. This will help to bring quietness and stillness to the soul and a release from the limitations and tensions of the everyday personality.

Now, gradually, focus upon the point of balance at the centre of the rhythms—the still flame in your heart which is beneath all thought, beneath all feeling, beneath all sound.... Visualize this flame as quite still, perhaps cradled in the shining heart of a flower, such as a pink or golden rose; and as you visualize, you will find that your breathing pattern is becoming slower and stiller, almost as if it were motionless. But do not strain to maintain this state, rather let it come naturally and rhythmically. God's rhythm is ordered and perfect.

Feel, as you breathe, that your whole body is becoming filled with light. Think of it as sunlight, sunshine, and that you are becoming filled with the sunlight from God; a ray from the Sun is shining right down into your heart and so onto the still flame, or the jewel, that is cradled there. Gradually now, as you breathe, you are withdrawing your consciousness from your outer self, from your body, from the lower mind of everyday and from the emotions. These are all becoming still and at peace, and fully under the control of your spirit, as your consciousness gently transfers itself from the outer world to the still centre of your being. Your physical senses remain quiescent, while the inner or etheric senses are becoming alert to experience the beauty of the inner world. From this point, your higher mind comes into play, both creatively and receptively.

*

The higher mind is very open to the suggestion of beauty, and it is here that the guiding voice of a teacher in a group, or the meditations outlined in chapter four, can help. As you use a meditation like the brief ones given, you will probably discover how the various elements—posture, breathing, use of the higher creative mind to visualize, to listen, to feel— all help you to withdraw from the outer, everyday world and to become aware instead of the inner world, the world of light.

Some people are fearful that in meditation they will find themselves out of control—that they will leave their body and be unable to return. Herein lies the reason for the careful ritual of bodily poise and relaxation. If you follow it faithfully, establishing from the outset your control over the temple that is your body, you need have no fear that you will go out of your body during meditation, or lose control of it, for your spirit has given its command and the body will obey; and with this sense of control, bodily discomforts, the aches and pains and coughs which can be so distracting, will recede utterly too.

It is also important, though, to 'come down to earth' again by gentle stages. If you feel as though you have been far away, in a very high or distant place, you may find it helps to get the feeling at the end that you are being gently taken down the hillside into a beautiful garden (White Eagle calls it 'the garden of reunion'). There you can rest for a while on Mother Earth, feeling her strength, and absorbing the beauty of the garden about you, while communing with loving souls, dear to you personally, who meet you in that garden. Then, when you are ready, 'breathe' your way back to full consciousness of your body, and when you really feel that you are fully back, mentally seal each psychic centre, or chakra. Seal them by visualizing the beautiful and powerfully protective symbol of the cross of light within the circle of light, as below, only composed of light:

See this, or mentally trace it, upon each centre.*

Then draw what we call the 'sevenfold breath'. That is to say, as you breathe in, imagine the light passing from the ground, through your left foot and up your left side to the crown of your head; and then breathe out, completing the circle down the right side. Do this seven times, really feeling yourself encircled by the beautiful protective light of life. Finally, on one breath, encircle the body in a spiral of light. As you breathe in, imagine the light passing in a spiral form around your body—seven times clockwise from the feet to the crown of the head; and then as

*The chakras are the seven energy centres of the body. For those unfamiliar with them, they are located as follows: at the very top of the head (the crown chakra); at the forehead (the brow chakra); in the hollow of the throat; at the heart (centrally within the chest, not necessarily in the physical heart); the solar plexus centre, situated above the navel; the spleen (under the 'floating ribs' at the back, on the left-hand side); and at the base of the spine. The chakras are centres of psychic energy which, in the physical body, are associated with important nerve centres and with the ductless glands. They are also linked, of course, with the etheric body and with all the subtler bodies of man, through which the gifts of the spirit will be able to manifest. White Eagle calls them 'the windows of the soul', for as they become awakened through meditation and aspiration, the aspirant becomes increasingly sensitive and aware of the inner world, and also more responsive to inspiration and guidance. The slightly simplified way they are given here is expanded in Joan Hodgson's book THE STARS AND THE CHAKRAS and Jenny Beeken's YOGA OF THE HEART, both published by The White Eagle Publishing Trust.

you breathe out, imagine the light going straight down from the top of the head, through the centre of the body, right down into the ground. Now you are well and truly earthed—'head in heaven, feet firmly on earth'.

Such a ritual of sealing need apply only to deep meditation or in a group situation when consciousness has been withdrawn from the physical for quite a period of time (you yourself will know when you have been really 'away'). Normally, when the contact has been briefer—like a short oasis in a busy day—it is sufficient just to breathe slowly, open the eyes and focus gradually on the world about you; when you feel that you are fully aware in your physical body, you may then choose to 'put on the whole armour of God' by mentally enfolding yourself with the equal-sided cross of light within the circle of light, on the sevenfold breath.

*

It is possible that as you begin to go more deeply into meditation (as is usually the case in a group situation) you may experience some physical sensation for which you cannot see any reason; for instance, a feeling of intense heat. I think it is best to take little notice of these sensations, for usually they pass, and are just an indication of some inner adjustment which is taking place. Sometimes, however, they can be the result of identifiable tension somewhere in the body and can be helped by re-examining the posture or mental attitude. Occasionally, for instance, pain is experienced at the back of the head: this is almost always due to tension. An attitude of quiet surrender, of quiet waiting upon God, rather than an eager trying, is usually the answer to this problem. Another way is deliberately to transfer the consciousness from the head to the heart centre. Think down into your heart, and the light that is shining there: picture the flower of the spirit which, like a beautiful rose, is opening to the sunlight. Discomfort at the back of the head can also occur if you come back into earth consciousness too quickly, but this won't happen if you carefully follow the 'coming down' procedure described. Make sure that you are really fully conscious at the physical level before sealing the chakras.

Part of the value of meditation is that it brings awareness of the existence of our subtler bodies beyond the physical one. It then enables us to identify our true self in full control of all the bodies. In the full sense of the word, we *realize* our true self. In meditation, and indeed in all spiritual work, the real 'I', the shining spirit, should be in full control, so that we only admit into the inner temple what we, the spirit, consciously or unconsciously know is right. While we are actually in meditation our spirit is in-

35

deed in control, even though the doors and windows of the soul are open to receive. Once we return to daily life, the earthly mind begins to take over; the spirit is no longer in such complete control. But if the chakras have been mentally sealed, there is no fear of intrusion by outside things such as other people's emotional energy, nor of our seeming to slip out of the body, or of our feeling a draining of energy. We remain master in the temple of our own being.

Remember that meditation is not the same as psychic development (the development of mediumistic or clairvoyant faculties), although meditation does develop an intuitive awareness in the aspirant. In meditation you do not at any time leave your body. Meditation is a controlled withdrawal of consciousness from the outer level to the innermost centre of your being, your own soul world. Ultimately, meditation is conscious union with God in you. It should give you more, not less, control over your body, your life and your day-to-day circumstances.

*

As a teacher of meditation I am sometimes asked if this 'earthing' of ourselves and sealing of the psychic centres in any way limits contact with our guide and teacher. The answer is no, except perhaps inasmuch as it ensures a pure and clear contact, undisturbed by forces from outside. Sealing takes place at the etheric level, but contact with the guide is on the plane of pure spirit. He or she speaks to you not from outside but within the stillness of your own heart's temple, and works with you through your higher self, to which you are eternally linked. As you meditate and become more and more aware of the spiritual life, putting spiritual principles into action in all you think and do, the link between the higher and lower self becomes progressively stronger until, as in the case of a master or great soul such as Jesus, the higher self is in almost total manifestation within the physical. Sealing the psychic centres in no way affects this link between the higher and the lower self.

Another question which arises is whether sealing the centres after healing or meditation would hinder a person's ability to send the light forth in healing. The answer is again no, for you are merely working at the etheric level to protect against unwanted intrusion from the emotional or astral level of life, and also against your 'clear vision' (clairvoyance in the broad sense) being awakened without it being under your control. Any giving must be a positive outgoing from the heart, directed by the spirit. The sealing of the centres actually makes it easier for you to radiate the light without distraction.

CHAPTER III

Help in visualizing

I HAVE ALREADY described how, in White Eagle's method of meditation, we use what he calls the higher, creative mind to visualize symbols of beauty, symbols which help us to still the busy mind and withdraw the consciousness from outer form to the inner reality of the spirit. Some find visualization quite easy, while others say they find it almost impossible. If you are one for whom it is a problem, don't be disheartened and feel, 'Oh, I will never get there'. With patience this faculty can be developed, and in my experience it is sometimes those who have the most difficulty in the early stages who in the end make the truest and most loving contact. Remember, too, that 'doing and seeing', valuable though it is, is not the be-all and end-all of meditation. The goal, as White Eagle says, is 'union with God-consciousness'; or, in the lovely symbolism of the East, the moment when 'the dewdrop slips into the shining sea'.

In other words, the lesser consciousness of the individual soul is absorbed into the whole. The ability to visualize and to use the inner senses helps you to reach this goal and to experience the inner worlds, but visualization is not an end in itself.

It is a mistake, too, to compare yourself with others in any such exercise, for you may experience as profound a soul lesson from one simple image, deeply felt, as another person will gain from an extended and complicated visionary experience. True soul experience can take place in a flash of time. Moreover, to regard what you *see* as all-important is to give priority to the sense of sight, not the deep inner awareness.

Often, difficulty in visualizing is associated with lack of observation at the earthly level—a lack of awareness of the world about you. Also, remember that in meditation you do not see objectively, or outside yourself; you see subjectively, within.

In the schools of old, a teacher would first train the pupil to use his or her powers of observation at the physical level. The teacher would place an object before the pupil and would bid him or her look at it very closely for some time. In the beginning, the object would be a very simple one, such as the little flame I described in an earlier chapter. Apart from its simplicity, the still flame is a very evocative symbol and its visualization a beautiful and effective way of finding the inner stillness.

As the pupil progressed they would be given a more subtle and complex object to observe, such as a perfect flower. The master would encourage the pupil to gaze intently upon the flower, impressing the whole image on his or her mind—the texture, shape and number of petals, the perfect blend of colour, the golden stamens, the sweet perfume; every detail was to be observed. And then the pupil had to close their eyes, and hold, for as long as they could, the mental image which had been printed on their consciousness. This would not be for very long in the early stages, but gradually the power to hold the image would increase.

This way of looking, this power truly to observe and see, was not only for the hours of meditation; it was to be practised constantly. In this way the pupil would gain the power of visualization gradually, quite independently of a physical object on which to concentrate. Later, perhaps, the pupil would be taught to awaken other senses. They would again be given some beautifully hand-wrought object or perhaps a piece of polished crystal, and would be taught to concentrate on the sense of touch. Alternatively, they would be helped to listen, or to recognize delicate scents. All the outer senses would be trained in this way. In your own meditation you may find it helpful to do this, or even to concentrate on holding some living object such as a tiny animal or bird, and really to experience the feeling evoked as you caress that form.

White Eagle tells us how young native Americans too were taught to observe and to listen, with their mind and heart, to all the sounds and sights of nature; and that thus they gradually learned to see and feel more than the outer form and to hear the inner voice of spirit.

Some people find that they can visualize quite happily when the image is described to them, either (if they are in a group) by the group leader, or as they read; but as soon as they are on their own, they seem to panic and can see no more. This is where the training in observation helps, because if you have trained yourself to look closely and observantly with the outer eye, it won't be difficult for you to do the same with your inner eye; and as you look for the detail, gradually the form will develop and unfold. Just be still and wait in love and worship.... Accept the beauty of the image that is before you, absorbing its beauty into yourself, and as you wait and look, gradually, to your surprise, you will find that more will unfold than your conscious mind suggests. You are then beyond the realm of 'it was just my imagination', and have reached the point where you are receptive to impressions and guidance from your own teacher in the inner world.

If, in spite of all, your power to visualize remains limited, don't be dismayed, for there is more than one way to the centre and it may be that you will be helped instead by the wise use of affirmations, or by mantras —the reciting or chanting of sacred sounds (but be careful over this, for chanting can be very powerful in its effect)—or by repeating words of aspiration silently in your heart, or even aloud. All these can help in the journey to the golden heart of the Sun, the still centre which is God. Most of us can at least visualize light, can imagine the glory of the Sun; so if, having prepared yourself as described, you can just sit quietly, breathing in the light, feeling yourself flooded and filled with it and enfolded in peace, you will still be doing very well. And, being filled, don't forget to share the blessing by thinking of humanity with love and compassion. Thus will the light flow from you.

Of course, there are other senses through which you can become aware of the world of spirit. Every physical sense has its finer counterpart, and in White Eagle's method of meditation he encourages us to develop and use all of them. For instance, he helps us to listen—to hear the harmony of nature, the music of the spheres, the voice of our teacher. And when we go, through our imagination, into the infinite and eternal garden of the spirit, if we listen, we can hear all the sounds of nature—the song of the birds, the sound of the running water, the beautiful musical sound of the wind in the trees. Yet if we listen even more deeply we can also hear the *inner* sound of all nature. White Eagle sometimes calls it the great *Aum*.... In the beginning was the Word: the Word of God, which resounds from the centre of the Sun. There can come a moment in meditation when you are caught up in that universal sound, which echoes from the tiniest grain of sand on the seashore to the farthest star.

Another sense with which we have been blessed is the sense of smell. The sense of smell is one of the finest and most evocative of the senses, and one through which, often, our brethren in the world of spirit are able to convey their presence, or a gift of the spirit, to our earthly consciousness. For instance, the fragrance of the rose, or of the tiny violet, may come to you; or you may in meditation have walked in the garden where the herbs grow, the rosemary, the thyme, the sage, and as you have inhaled those fragrances, some special blessing or quality of spirit has come to your heart.

Then there is the sense of taste. You are aware of it

if the sharing of the bread and the wine in communion is part of your meditation, as it is in the White Eagle services, or when, in your meditation, you cup your hands in the running water of the crystal stream and drink the water and your soul is refreshed. You taste the light in the crystal water, you taste its purity. Again, you are learning to become aware in the inner worlds.

Finally there is the sense of touch. When you visualize and go into the infinite and eternal garden, and perhaps stand by a strong tree, you may lay your hands upon it and feel the texture of the bark, and embrace the tree and feel its strength and commune with its living spirit. Or, as you touch Mother Earth, you feel her strength and how generous she is, and you feel love for her. You feel too the softness of the grass beneath your feet: again you are experiencing through the senses of your spirit.

The growing awareness that this awakens in you will help you very much in your human relationships, too, for it will help you to realize that you are not separate from your brother or sister, but part of him or her—even as your experience in the garden is helping you to *become* that which you see, to become one with the tree, one with the tiny flower at your feet, one with the sound of the running water, to breathe with the tiny creature in your hand, to breathe with Mother Earth.

Now, truly, the time will come when you don't need to go into meditation in the conventional sense to do these things, because as you walk in your garden and you open your inner ears, you will hear those beautiful inner sounds, you will become aware of those in the world of spirit walking in the garden with you—aware of the spirits of the trees, yes, and even of the angels. Ultimately your meditation will become your way of life.

But it all begins with learning how to be still. It all begins and it all ends with becoming aware of the spirit, becoming aware that you *are* spirit. Love the body which God has given you, for God has given you this temple of your being through which to work and serve and experience on earth. Your physical body should be cared for, loved—I would almost say reverenced. But remember that it is not the real you, for you are shining spirit; the body is an instrument that you have helped to build through your experiences of many lives past; it has been given to you as a gift from God, through which to serve, to experience and to learn.

The same applies to your mind, your mental body. The mind of earth can be so tiresome: it can hold us, limit us, limit our horizons, and yet it is a valuable tool which we have to learn to use. In the course of our experience in meditation we learn to use a higher aspect of the mind, a higher mind, a mind which is free—a mind which, as we have already learnt, we can use to create form, to create beauty, to create a beautiful temple of the spirit. Still another gift from God is your emotional body. It holds emotions which can be exhausting and wearying, and which can make us do such foolish things sometimes; but it can also, under the control of the spirit, be a power which can stimulate and give the strength to achieve.

White Eagle guides us to love all levels of our being, but also to become aware of ourselves as shining, strong and beautiful spirit, greatly loved. We, as spirit, came forth from the heart of God. In the end, which is also a beginning, we shall return to the heart from which we came.

*

How we can know where, in meditation, visualization or imagination ends and true vision starts, is a question often asked. To find the answer, perhaps we should again remind ourselves of the real purpose and goal of our meditation, which is to find the place of deep stillness and peace within our own innermost being, where the jewel of truth lies—the jewel of the Christ-spirit within the lotus of the heart. What is it that White Eagle says?

Through meditation and quiet contemplation the

outer layers of the mind and emotion are gradually laid aside and man rests in the innermost place of stillness where the jewel of truth lies, the jewel within the lotus of his heart. This is the light which lighteth every man, the Christ, the Son of God in him.... The mind must be stilled, and the spirit must become aware, must become conscious of its being. Then the soul of man becomes illumined with divine spirit and consciousness expands into worlds of beauty and truth which bring peace and joy to the human soul.

from THE STILL VOICE, pp. 1–2

As I have already said, White Eagle helps us to still the unruly mind and emotions by guiding us to concentrate first upon breathing, and then by a process of visualization. Through visualizing forms of beauty as he has taught us to do, we gradually reach that place of inner stillness and purity where no breath of thought or emotion disturbs the still lake of our consciousness.

For instance, we may visualize the quiet pool in the centre of the garden of peace, upon which there floats the perfect form of a pure white lotus or lily flower, and within its heart, the diamond, the blazing jewel. Or perhaps we may see that living centre as a dewdrop—it can take many forms. But we can become so absorbed in contemplation of this won-der that all the activity of the everyday mind ceases. We are just absorbed into, and so become part of, the jewel, or the dewdrop. It is, as it were, a state of suspended thought and being into which we have entered. This is the point at which conscious imagination ceases, and spontaneous vision and awareness begin. It is as though the soul becomes a shining mirror in which truth is reflected. Then the vision begins to open without any conscious direction on the part of the aspirant. It is not that you say to yourself, 'I will visualize a temple, or a garden, or a fountain of light': you just find your vision unfolding, your consciousness expanding, in the world of light.

What comes to you then is a true reflection, in your soul world, of truth from God, and it is beyond conscious thought or imagination on your part. It could be that your guide and teacher, quite unconsciously to you, is using your higher mind to reveal images of beauty through which you will gain understanding, or which will awaken certain qualities in you which you need for your life's journey.

Whether you feel you reach this point or not, White Eagle suggests that we should never decry visualization or say, 'Oh, it is only our imagination'. Remember, it is not so much what you see or visualize in meditation that is important, as what the vision conveys to your heart, what feeling or understanding stirs within you as you gaze upon that form which you are visualizing. Remember too that to visualize is to *create*, for you are bringing into operation the creative power of your higher mind, and the form created is a real and living form. Nevertheless, as I have already said, although you may think that what you are seeing or experiencing is just the result of your own conscious direction, very often—indeed, nearly always—this thought has been put into your higher mind by your guide and teacher who, without you recognizing it, is guiding your footsteps according to your soul's need, and is leading you into the inner world.

CHAPTER IV

Some meditations to use as seed thoughts

1 : THE LOTUS POOL

AS YOU SIT, quietly withdrawing your consciousness from the outer world to the still place within, the place which is all light, you see (or are shown by your guide or teacher) the symbol of a beautiful archway of light. You cannot see what lies beyond the archway, except that it is bathed in golden sunlight, and you long to go through to find what lies beyond.

Now you find that you are being gently led forward, towards and through the arch into the world beyond. At first you cannot see form; all you are aware of is the light. But then, little by little, you become aware that you are in a beautiful garden, what White Eagle calls 'the infinite and eternal garden'. There is a wonderful sense of new life springing up everywhere; even the grass and the earth beneath your feet feel vibrant and alive, and give you a feeling of strength and new life. Yet all is gentle: there is a deep underlying peace and calm ... the peace of eternity.

When you are ready, feel that you are being gently led through the garden to a still pool, whereon floats a pure white lotus or water lily, its petals opening to the Sun; you sense and feel the life—God—in every shining petal and in its golden heart. There is a clear jewel, like a wondrous diamond, cradled there. Be very still before this beauty....

It may be that as you sit beside the pool in quiet contemplation, breathing into your heart the gentle purity and perfume of the lovely flower, you will find yourself in the presence of one who loves you, your guide and teacher. He or she speaks words of wisdom to your heart.

When you are ready, gradually bring yourself back to consciousness of the world about you.

2 : A COMMUNION WITH OUR TEACHER

HAVING ATTUNED yourself, at the start of the meditation, to the still place within, imagine that you are sitting by the quiet lake among the mountains; the lake is still and shining, and as you sit there by the shore you absorb peace into your soul, and sunshine. All is tranquillity and happiness.

Now look up and see the mountains which rise out of the valley. One particularly calls; it is snowcapped but shining golden in the sunlight. You know you have to ascend the mountain, for something tells you that your teacher is there, waiting. The climb is not easy, but you are helped every step of the way—even, it seems, carried on eagle's wings to that golden peak. Yes, your teacher is there, all love, and clad so simply. He or she speaks gently and to your heart words of both kindness and wisdom; or maybe you just bask in the aura of this dear teacher and are lifted in consciousness right into the light....

For a while, you may like to commune with those you love in the world of spirit. Your teacher will tell you when it is time to return, and you then turn your face again towards the valley and come quietly down. Breathe in the gentle air, and thus slowly breathe your way right back to consciousness of the world about you and your physical body.

3 : THE TEMPLE OF THE TREES

OPEN YOUR consciousness first to the gentle influence of our teacher, White Eagle. He is taking us to the temple of the trees. The trees can be your own favourites, the ones which most speak a message to your heart. But he leads you first along a path between the pines....

You can hear the magic of the wind among their branches and feel the warm pine needles beneath your feet as you walk. After a time you come to an open space, circular in shape—your temple of the trees—and sit quietly there for a while, absorbing the beauty and eternal strength of the trees, which form a protective circle about you, and breathe with them. Gradually you become aware of many little creatures of the woods joining you—all very friendly and not in the least afraid, as they feel your love.

As you meditate here, one comes to you who is all light: comes with great love, lifts you to your feet and leads you along a path of light into the Sun.... Your temple of trees has become the temple of the Sun, and brethren of all time are gathered here in loving communion....

When you are ready, retrace your steps, back to earthly consciousness, but filled with the light of the Sun.

4 : THE MASTER JESUS

This beautiful vision was given to us by Minesta.

LET US try to attune ourselves to the presence and influence of Jesus. He comes to us in meditation in the heart of an immense Sun—Star, in a beautiful human form, clothed in white, girdled with gold, and with golden sandals on his feet. From his eyes divine love streams. The expression upon his face conveys the wisdom of ages. Sometimes he appears to step out of the Star and with arms stretched forth comes towards us with loving greeting. He is, then, the Elder Brother who understands human life and its need for comfort, guidance and strength.

It is essentially this human personality which becomes so dear to us; for not only does he appear to be one with us, a companion and friend of our earthly life, but shining through his face and form is the heavenly Christ light, which makes the human form appear transparent as the Sun light illumines and radiates all around it.

To see him like this is to be utterly, completely convinced of the reality and truth of spiritual life and power operative behind physical matter. He is the instrument of the supreme light of life, the Godhead.

5 : A HEALING MEDITATION

'THE ANCIENTS saw and worshipped the Sun as sign and symbol of God, and called upon the spiritual sunlight for strength, help and healing. So let us also call....' (*words from the White Eagle Absent Healing Service*)

Sitting quietly with spine held gently upright but in no way stiff, with shoulders peacefully relaxed so that the arms feel almost heavy, with the back of the neck also gently stretched, but with the eyes looking down towards the heart, become aware of the gentle inflowing and outflowing of the breath. For a few moments, focus your whole attention on this gentle peaceful rhythm, feeling as you breathe that you are breathing in the breath of God.

Say the healing prayer:

'Sunlight of life and being, of health, vitality and all creativeness, flood us and fill us … fill us … fill us….

'We are now become as flames of Thee, golden light of the heavens, heavenly radiance and illumination.'

Peacefully and gently hold this still radiance of the Sun deep in your heart-mind; with every gentle breath feel that radiance gradually permeating every cell of the physical body, melting away any pain, tension or inharmony. (In no way focus on the inharmony, but always on the radiance of the Christ Sun.)

As you rest in this stillness, draw into the heart of the Christ Sun–Star any soul you know to be in need of healing, any country or tragic situation which you particularly feel the urge to help. Keep on with the quiet peaceful breathing, and with all the strength of your spirit call upon the angels of the Sun, the great healing angels, to enfold the person or the condition you are trying to help in wings of light and healing.

Of ourselves we can do nothing; but as soon as we become still and attuned to the Christ Sun within, we are united with a great company, both human and angelic, who are working to bring into being the harmony, the healing, the brotherhood of the new age. By our true prayer and meditation we become channels for the light.

6 : A MEDITATION ON THE CHRISTMAS TREE

This is particularly suitable as a group meditation.

LET US commence with the feeling that we are being drawn gently upwards towards and into a bright Star of Bethlehem. It is shining above our heads like the Pole Star of our innermost being, or the Christ Star.

Peacefully and gently we breathe in the light of the Christ Star; and we now feel ourselves becoming one with a little Christmas tree in a quiet wood. We are conscious of our feet becoming roots, going deep into the earth and drawing up the nourishment, the sap of earth-experience, which gradually builds the tree of life in us. We are aware of the quiet life of the forest, almost of the inbreathing and outbreathing of Mother Earth in the coldness and resting state of midwinter. And then the Star above our heads becomes more radiant and ablaze with light and we are aware of the song of the angels of the Star. The Star becomes ever brighter as the angels rejoice at the birth of the Christ in the hearts of all people.

From this blazing Star and the song of the angels, we become aware of the quickening of the earth around the roots of the tree. The light of the Star pours down into the earth and the roots of the tree then draw up that light, through the trunk of the tree, radiating it through the branches until the whole tree is radiant with the Star light. On the branches now there shine lights of many colours, gifts of the spirit for humanity.

For a few moments our tree basks in this radiance. Christmas bells and angel voices create a song of joy and peace. We are now part of a great Christmas tree of light, reaching right from the earth into the heaven-world, where there is a wonderful celebration, an eternal ceremony of the rebirth of the Christ Son in the hearts of all people. In this temple of the Christ Mass are many happy children of all nations, gathered round the tree in a joyful, homely company, all reunited with parents or spiritual guardians—a joyful company, singing praises, enjoying the beautiful gifts of the spirit which come to them from the great Christmas tree of light.

Crowning the tree, an angel of the Star brings a deep stillness and a sense of worship into every heart, as we are raised in consciousness into the simple cave, the birthplace of the newborn babe. All the revelry subsides as each child—and we are all children—is led to worship at the manger....

The deep peace and love which fills our being radiates out as a great healing light to bless first of all those near and dear to us, and gradually spreading to encompass the world....

CHAPTER V

A look at problems which arise

BEGINNERS in creative meditation often feel that they are standing outside and looking on instead of being involved in what they see. They see, but they do not 'feel'.

There are several ways of getting beyond this difficulty, though they all come back to the same truth, that of 'becoming that which you see'. For instance, you are meditating upon the infinite and eternal garden, and you try to experience it with all your inner senses—you inhale the perfume of the flowers, you taste the crystal waters of the stream, you listen to the music of the wind in the trees, you touch the trunk of the tree, feeling its strength. You lean back against the tree.... But then, can you begin to feel the life of the tree, grow with it, feel that you are part of it? Can you feel your roots reaching down to draw sustenance from Mother Earth, and your branches reaching skywards, spreading out under the Sun? As you put your feet into the water and feel its cool touch, can you be absorbed into the water, becoming part of it, flowing with it? Can you surrender utterly into the heart of the Sun, and feel no heat, only oneness? Can you look on the tiny blade of grass and feel that the God in you is one with the God, the light, in that tiny green blade? Can you grow with it, feel with it, be the light in it? Can you touch the soft feathers of the bird, feel the bird's tiny heartbeat as you hold it to your heart and know it to be part of God as you yourself are part of God, sharing a spark of the divine?

Another way you can learn to experience full involvement is in the following meditation.

Create with your higher mind a perfect flower, shall we say a single rose—perfect in form, colour and fragrance—with a shining jewel at its centre?

Then, see a pure ray of sunshine pouring upon that jewel and reflecting from it in dazzling colours. Gaze upon this lovely flower, cup it in your hands, then take it right into your heart so that where the ray from the Sun is pouring into your heart, there too are the flower and the jewel. There will be no need for thought then; the 'running commentary' of the lower mind, from which it is usually so difficult to get away, will be stilled, for you will just *be* in the light, absorbing it and reflecting it, wholly at peace, and filled with joy. You will not want to move from that place. In other words, you will have found and become the still centre.

Those of you who were blessed enough to meditate with White Eagle speaking through his instrument, Minesta, will know that again and again he would lead us into meditation upon the Golden One, or upon the Great Healer, 'He who is all love'; and that in communion with Him, in His presence, we were filled with love. Our hearts were stirred and we found ourselves drawn into His very being, becoming part of Him, and there was now no dividing thought, only love and being in the light.

This meditation on, and absorption into, the being of the Master, be it the Christ, or the Buddha, is another way to cross from being an observer to being totally involved in what you see in meditation.

*

We move on to another problem which arises, particularly when first setting out on the spiritual path, or starting regular meditation: it is so easy to become discouraged, to think that we are making no progress. We all go through these periods. However, White Eagle teaches us that it is a mistake to think in terms of progress or lack of it on the spiritual path, for this suggests a narrow absorption with oneself—which is the very antithesis of the true spiritual life. The saints of old did not set out to become saints, they set out to love and serve; they set out to do a certain piece of work, fired by the love of God. Perhaps we should forget progress and think simply in terms of loving and serving and being: above all, of practising the presence of God. In any case, who are we to judge the state of our souls, still less the state of the souls of our brothers? We can but 'keep on keeping on' trying; and undoubtedly continual discipline is needed, for it is so easy to fall into the trap of laziness on the spiritual path, particularly when we do become a little discouraged through apparent lack of progress.

We need constantly to make the effort to withdraw from worldliness if we are to become useful servants of the great Master. For, as White Eagle says: 'Only this will give you the power to do those little acts of service that the Master asks of you' (MEDITATION, p. 161).

It is good to have the courage to 'look in the mirror' in meditation and accept ourselves as we are; and to see those things that can be changed, to enable us to reflect more of God into the world; but not to be discouraged when we look in the mirror and see the same old blemish still there—rather to keep on keeping on, with renewed dedication.

A beautiful symbol is that of the seed in the dark earth. You sow the seed, and for quite a long time—interminably it seems, sometimes—nothing happens. And then one bright day a little tender, green, curved shoot appears. All through those long weeks of waiting and watering your seed, something was happening underneath in the dark earth, though you could not see it. Roots were pushing down to draw sustenance from the earth and give strength to the little shoot that was pushing up towards the light.

So it may be that in those times when we feel depressed with our progress, something is happening deep within, in the darkness: roots are going down which are going to sustain the flower and fruit in due season, and in the end bring forth the golden harvest.

*

Another problem, not unconnected with this one, is to feel inadequate when sitting with others in a group, because the others in the group seem to do and experience so much; while you, apparently, do so little. White Eagle teaches us, though, that the value of meditation is not to be judged by the amount seen and experienced, but rather (if it is to be judged at all) by the amount 'felt', by the depth of stillness and worship, the discipline of body, mind and emotions, and the extent to which each aspirant is able to give themselves utterly into the light. The contemplation of a single shining dewdrop or a stretch of calm and sunlit water may convey more to the heart than a whole landscape of experience. So don't try to match yourself with others. Begin slowly; don't try to run before you can walk. Instead of trying to 'see' and 'do', content yourself for a while with the first simple step which is both the beginning and end of meditation. Just have a 'Sun bathe'. That is to say, close your eyes and imagine that you are gazing into the heart of the heavenly Sun, warm and golden, and that you are enfolded in its glorious rays.... A ray from the heart of the Sun is shining down into your heart; perhaps you may even see or feel the beautiful rose opening in your heart as the Sun's ray shines down into it. Say inwardly, or aloud if you can, again and again, 'God is in me.... Divine light shines in me; light from the heart of the Sun shines in me and floods and fills every atom of my being.'

Imagine this happening, and that the ray of light from the Sun from which your whole being is filled is centred upon your heart. This will cause your heart centre to stir and, almost before you can be conscious of the process, will give you a feeling of your relationship with the great light in the heavens: God, the Father–Mother. There will be times when you feel drawn right up into the light.

When you have persisted faithfully with this simple exercise for a little while, try to visualize the tiny flame in the heart of the Sun. Hold it very still before you, as you breathe gently and quietly. Hold your mind still, too, so that no breath of thought gives movement to the flame. Then, see that still flame in the centre of the Sun, brighter and purer even than the Sun itself. Know that this little flame is the essence of God in you, your spirit, part of the great Sun. Affirm: 'I AM one with the infinite Sun, forever and forever and forever....'

You may possibly be helped to make contact with the heart of the Sun, by using the power of the Word as described in the book MEDITATION (p. 131). Having taken a deep breath, very quietly chant the sound, the *Aum*, thinking all the time of God, and of the still centre of all life. The very vibration of the sound will take you ever further into the light, into the heart of the Sun. You can worship there for as long as you feel able to remain in that state. This won't be for very long at first, but you will feel greatly refreshed from this beautiful contact in the Sun. Don't forget to seal yourself afterwards, by imagining a cross of light within a circle of light ⊕ upon each of the brow, throat, heart and solar plexus centres, and then by seeing your whole body encircled by light.

Your guide and teacher understands your earnest aspiration to be a true brother of the light, and in the fullness of time you will reap the reward of all your efforts.

A problem for some is the thought of losing their individuality as they 'merge into the Supreme'. They don't like the idea of being swallowed up into eternal unity with everything else. 'Surely our individualization is important?', they say.

From what I have learnt from White Eagle, I do not believe for a moment that union with God implies loss of individuality; in any case I can absolutely assure those who have that fear that they will lose neither personality nor individuality while they are clinging to them! I believe that individualization is indeed important, otherwise why should we have been breathed forth with separate egos, to take the long journey through all manner of experience in matter, eventually to become men and women perfected, Christed ones?

We think the question arises from a misunderstanding of what is meant by union with God and all life. Perhaps it will help us to understand if we realize that, as White Eagle says, 'life is consciousness'.

The soul in incarnation is, in the beginning, very limited in its consciousness. Its awareness does not extend much beyond the physical body, the conditions of physical life, and its needs. Then, with an awakening and growing intelligence, it reaches out, its consciousness expanding to embrace mental concepts and ideas; there comes a response not only to physical stimuli but to subtler stimuli such as the beauty of music—or beauty in any form. Through pain and suffering, and perhaps through joy too, sympathy, understanding and imagination dawn, so that the soul begins to feel for and with another; the earlier concentration on its own immediate needs broadens to an awareness of the needs of others. Consciousness expands further as the soul begins to see life through another's eyes. Every deep experience in life, be it of joy or sorrow, brings what we may call an initiation, which is a transformation of consciousness.

There comes a point when the feet are consciously set upon the spiritual path, and the process of expanding consciousness is hastened. Through aspiration and meditation, the soul gradually becomes aware of another world, a world of light, permeating the solid matter in which it is clothed, and which until now it had thought was the whole of life. The man–woman becomes aware of life as spirit, as light permeating all matter.... In meditation, consciousness may expand outside time, so that the past, the present and even the future are all experienced as one. Above all the soul becomes increasingly aware of the Christ light within itself and in all people, and knows this light to be part of God, part of the glory of the Sun; begins to realize this not just with the mind but with the whole being; realizes that all is in the One, the

One in all; and that truly we are all part of one another, as we are all part of God.

The soul can, in meditation, become utterly absorbed into this glory, apparently losing identity; and
yet it does not do so, for it always remains aware and
awareness must mean individuality. 'I think, therefore I am.' A master soul, we think, can remain in
this universal consciousness or withdraw into a more
individualized form at will. For most of us, the universal consciousness is a glimpse, a flash of what it
might be, caught in moments of exaltation. But the
bliss we feel at that moment stirs within us a long for
conscious union with God, which is thenceforth the
goal of our aspiration.

CHAPTER VI

Some further questions

THE QUESTIONS in this chapter are not all directly connected with meditation, but all have arisen out of meditational experience.

Can you explain the difference between psychic development and meditation?

We would say that in the first you are developing just one aspect of your manifold being, but that meditation in its true state, when attained, illumines the soul at every level of consciousness. This total illumination, and the love for God and His creation which comes with it, will always be the true goal of the aspirant. Psychic development can be achieved without meditation, but you will never achieve through psychic development alone the expansion of consciousness, or the deep peace, the renewed life and health and the happiness in everyday living that meditation can bring. What is more, you can and do contact your loved ones in meditation, and enjoy a true and beautiful companionship with them.

When White Eagle takes us into meditation, he first takes us right up to the heights of worship and helps us to be absorbed in the great light; and then, when we are ready, brings us gently down through the planes of consciousness and helps us to see and to feel at a level he calls 'the garden of reunion'. Here, in this beautiful garden, we can walk and talk with those we love and hold true communion with them. We speak to them mentally, they hear our thoughts and we hear theirs, either directly (that is to say, we mentally hear them speak, even as surely as if we heard the physical voice) or what they are saying will slip into our minds and we will know the message to be theirs. They have their own way, too, of proving by small incidents in everyday life, that it is not 'just imagination'—that they really are there.

Such a contact in the garden of reunion is real, and can be deeply satisfying. Moreover, constant communion in this way helps to 'thin the veil' so that we become more aware in daily life of the interpenetration of the two worlds, and that truly there is no separation; that *all life is one*.

Psychic development may be, and indeed would inevitably be at some stage, a part of this wider expansion of consciousness; but it can be, and often is, limited to development at the astral level, so that the would-be medium is seeing into an astral world only—a world which, albeit very beautiful, is still subject to conflict and illusion, being quite close to the earth. The medium who has developed the higher consciousness of which we have been speaking can pass right through those lower planes of illusion and see eternal truth, but if this higher consciousness has not been developed, the vision is limited and liable to confusion and error.

There are certain people who have come back to the earth with the special mission to be a bridge between the two worlds. Their subtler bodies are so constructed and attuned that contact with the world of spirit is easy for them; their gift, once developed and wisely used, enables them to make the most beautiful and true contact and become splendid instruments of guidance and teaching from the highest level to those on earth. However, mediumship of this kind is limited to the few: those, as we say, with a special mission to fulfil. Not everyone is a potential medium, but everyone, without exception, can build his or her own bridge into consciousness of the inner worlds of eternal life, through meditation as taught by White Eagle, and by the methods taught by great teachers through the ages.

I have been meditating regularly now for some time, and a friend mentioned that sometimes the opposition tries to get at you and stop you progressing—is this true?

When we consciously set out on a path of spiritual service and aspiration, in a way this does intensify the forces which can pull us off the path. But it is generally a mistake to think of these forces as being outside ourselves, for really it is our own lower selves which seem to rise up with renewed vigour to tempt us off the path.

The writer speaks of the 'opposition', a term which I take to mean the forces of darkness, or 'brothers of the shadow'. I think it would be more true to say that when we first set our feet on the spiritual path we are tested. Just as, when young, right through from the beginning of our schooling until we pass out of the education system, we have to sit for examinations; so on the spiritual path trials come along from time to time (sometimes so thick and fast that we are almost tempted to give up!). They are trials which measure the strength of the spirit in us. Are we going to be steadfast and true to the path on which we have set our feet, or are we going to become fearful and give up? We are also tested for certain qualities of the spirit—for discernment, discrimination, desirelessness, dispassion, faith, wisdom, humility, and many other qualities which, when attained, will make us better servants of God (and much happier people in ourselves). Above all we are tested for the quality of our love for God and for our brothers.

It sometimes seems as though the testing—the 'opposition', if you like—comes from a force outside ourselves, but as we said earlier the real tempter is within and is the voice of the lower self. There are forces of darkness, but they can only work through the weakness in ourselves; and by the same token they can always be overcome by the strength of the Christ within. As White Eagle says, 'The noble Christ-self in you rises up to overcome the tempter'; and every time this happens the Christ-self is thereby strengthened.

In the old days the forces of darkness would be equated with the devil, or with Satan, but (again as White Eagle says),

Satan is only another word for Saturn, the tester; and even the negative force is slowly and painfully working in life to test and purify the soul, and eventually to bring wisdom, bring light, bring out all that is finest in the nature. With these great beings of darkness you are only seeing one side of their work; but the reverse side is vastly different and they have a purpose in creating the perfect jewel from the rough stone.

The best way to combat forces of darkness and the

weakness inherent in ourselves is to be absolutely strong and steadfast in the light, concentrating only on the light and on all that is good. When the mind is filled with God and with the light, the brothers of the shadow can have no entry. It is another way of saying, 'to put on the whole armour of God'.

In some tapes and books on meditation there is the reminder that the chakras must be closed afterwards; in others there is never a mention of such things. For a long time I did not know of this closing technique and came to no harm. It was the same when giving healing. Many say you must close your own and the sick person's chakras afterwards. I did not do this for years. Again I did not seem to suffer any unpleasant after-effects. Some people say it is out-of-date and old-fashioned to go through all that closing-down performance. I get very confused.

It is true that some people perhaps put a lot of unnecessary anxiety into sealing the chakras after healing and meditation. On the other hand, some need this conscious sealing more than others, being by nature more open and receptive, and it is better to be safe than sorry. In the White Eagle healing work it is by no means uncommon for people to come for help because they have ignorantly opened the chakras through some form of psychic or occult dabbling, or a half-understood form of meditation, without any knowledge of how to seal themselves. Such people can be in a sorry state and it often takes much time and application before their equilibrium is restored.

A good deal must depend on the level, or depth, of meditation. Meditation is a term rather loosely used, as we have seen, inasmuch as it can cover anything from the five minutes spent in stillness and prayer or in 'sending out the light', to a prolonged state of profound inner awareness and detachment from the physical world. To reach this latter condition it may even be that some form of chanting or other practice has been used. Always, always in these cases it is best for the meditator to come back to physical awareness deliberately and slowly, through the planes of consciousness, and to seal each chakra, before taking up his or her duties in the outer world. Indeed, any meditative state where deep heart-contact has truly been made, and awareness of the physical world has almost receded, even if only for a short period of time, should be followed by sealing. The meditator should be able to judge for him or herself how far removed from earth consciousness and how receptive he or she has been. But it is better to seal when it isn't necessary than to fail to seal when it is. A feeling of slight detachment, a queer feeling at the back of the head, a feeling of being edgy and irritable, or weary and drained: these are all signs of your having 'left the doors open', and that you need to be more careful. Meditation should leave you feeling strong and vitalized and happy.

With regard to sealing yourself after healing, again this depends to some extent on the condition of the patient and the circumstances. The really important thing is for the healer to immerse hands (and if possible forearms) in cold water after each treatment. But sometimes the inexperienced healer may suffer from a draining from the solar plexus which is due to emotional involvement in the case, and trying to give too much of themselves (rather than leaving it to God and the angels). If you feel this draining, it is advisable to seal the solar plexus after giving treatment. In the White Eagle healing we always conclude the treatment by sealing the throat and solar plexus centres of the patient.

May we add that a sure way to get into a spiritual tangle is to try to follow more than one teacher or method at one and the same time? When the pupil first consciously sets foot on the spiritual path, there is usually a period of searching and, to some extent, experimenting. But after a while, if the pupil is an earnest seeker and searches with their heart as well as with their mind, suddenly they will know that they are 'home'. They will know, 'This is it.... This is my path'. No doubt, quite unconsciously to them, they have been led to the path by their own guide. Having found their chosen teacher, they would be wise, if they really wish to touch the deeper levels of consciousness and to become a true and valuable server, to follow the path unswervingly and with utter faithfulness. By this stage they cannot mix methods without, at the least, wasting time, and at the most, opening themselves to risk. White Eagle opens for us all a path of spiritual unfoldment and of spiritual healing which is absolutely safe providing you follow it exactly. If you have accepted White Eagle as your teacher, and you practise his method of meditation, then always seal the centres after deep meditation, in the way described on pp. 32–34, above.

There is nothing old-fashioned about this sealing technique except that it is, in essence, part of the Ancient Wisdom; rituals of a similar nature will, I believe, long continue to have their place in spiritual unfoldment for those who aspire to touch ever deepening levels of consciousness.

We are taught on the one hand that we must learn to enter into the feelings of another; yet at the same time we are told to be dispassionate. How can we be both? What is meant by being dispassionate?

We think that the best answer to this problem, as with so many problems on the spiritual path, is to try to imagine what the Master would do in similar circumstances. The Master would, we think, be full of compassion for the suffering of those around them, full of understanding and deep tenderness; feeling with the sufferer, but not allowing himself to be pulled into the emotional storm because he knows that this would weaken his power to help.

A master's love, as well as being human, is divine. A master knows with all his being the great and eternal love of God which always brings joy out of sorrow, light out of darkness, peace after pain. He (or she) has the perspective to see that out of the suffering and pain, wisdom and happiness will arise. Remaining calm and all love, emotions stilled and (like the still lake) reflecting the Sun, he becomes for the sufferer a reminder of the love of God which comforts, uplifts and heals. But if he were to allow himself to become emotionally disturbed the waters of the lake would be ruffled: he would be doubting God's love and therefore no longer be able to reflect it.

It is indeed difficult for us, when we first set out on the spiritual path, to find the point of balance between dispassion on the one hand, and feeling with our brother on the other. We become, in the early stages, very sensitive and easily hurt, both on our own account and for others, and even more ruled by emotion than we have previously been. But gradually, as we 'keep on keeping on' we get beyond that stage.

When the God in us takes control, the mind and emotions become our tools instead of our being ruled by them.

Constant meditation on, and aspiration to communion with, the Master Jesus, the Great Healer, is a very great help in this matter; for from it there grows in the heart not sentiment, nor uncontrolled and therefore weakening emotion, but an overwhelming awareness of the love of God and of the quality of that love. We see, for a moment, through the eyes of the Master and know nothing but a love which is wise. It is personal, in the sense that it is a deeply tender understanding of every one of God's creatures; but it is also dispassionate, embracing all things equally, because it recognizes the harmony and perfection of God's plan for His creation, and that God always brings light out of darkness.

We think that dispassionate love is that which truly has no touch of self in it.

Can you please outline the duties of (1) the guardian angel and (2) the guide?

We don't think that either the guide or the guardian angel has 'duties' as such, for theirs is a service born of love. In the case of the guardian angel, it is a divine, heavenly love, peaceful, and not ruled by emotion. We feel that the guardian angel comes to the child very much on the ray of Divine Mother. In fact White Eagle himself says:

> The guardian angel, as well as the form, the influence of Divine Mother, is always present at the time of birth. Always the guardian angel cares for that soul reincarnating, and the Divine Mother's love is helping the process of that physical birth. The birth even of the smallest creature is a heavenly manifestation of an invisible power and is attended by angels.

from SPIRITUAL UNFOLDMENT 2, p. 53

White Eagle also says that the guardian angel is the 'guardian of the law', the karmic law which rules all life. Every soul comes back into incarnation with a certain karmic pattern to fulfil, a certain path to tread. The task of the guardian angel is to bring the soul in its charge into the very situation and condition where the lesson of its karma may be learnt, to bring to it the very experience the soul asked for while still in the heavenly, illumined state before it came into incarnation. Again, in White Eagle's words, 'The guardian of the law (the guardian angel) watches over, records and guides the outworking of the karmic law, the law of cause and effect, in the life of the soul'.

A beautiful part of the meditational experience is the soul's growing awareness of the guardian angel.

In leading a group meditation, I am often aware of the angel guardian of each individual sitter in the group. At first it appears as if the angel is just behind the sitter, with wings of light outspread; the whole group is within the protective circle of angelic beings. Then, gradually, as the work proceeds, it is as though each sitter is at the centre of that being of light which is their angel, surrounded by and enfolded in light and thus protected from disquieting thoughts and outside influences.

As the soul progresses on the spiritual path, and begins to be able to quieten the mind, and when the emotions and passions are stilled and disciplined, then the soul becomes increasingly conscious of the heavenly form and protective wings of the guardian angel lifting it towards the Sun. This awareness of the guardian angel is a most beautiful and strengthening experience.

With regard to the guide, let us realize first that this being is not of the angelic stream of life, but is a human companion, one with whom the soul has links from the past, perhaps has known through many lives. This beautiful and loving spirit knows you well, perhaps better even than you know yourself until you can see with clear vision, for your guide knows, where you probably cannot, the pattern of your karma and the lessons to be learned. The task of your guide is quite literally to guide you, to teach you, to lead you to the source of the wisdom your soul needs at a particular time—to inspire and help at every level.

To understand the work of the guide, you need to have caught a glimpse, a vision, of the meaning of brotherhood; for all souls of all time are not separate but part of one another, and there is a great brotherhood of illumined souls dedicated to serving, leading and loving their brethren still in incarnation as they make their long journey back to the centre from which they came.

These illumined brethren come back because they love humanity, they love the soul in their care with a love which we on earth can scarcely comprehend. Think of this great brotherhood, each one of whom has himself or herself been through the same trials, tests and joys that we on earth experience. Think of them withdrawing a little from their state of perfect harmony and drawing close to those on earth who have been given into their care, and to whom they are drawn by links of friendship and karma extending, maybe, over many lives. The one on earth, perhaps, is unconscious of that loving guidance; but as he or she, guided invisibly by the one in spirit, consciously sets foot on the spiritual path (as all must in the end do), there is a gradual awakening as the soul on earth begins to become aware, responding more and more to the guidance, to the loving companionship. On occasion the guide will work through someone dear to the soul but on the other side of life. Whatever the case, no soul is ever left to travel the path of life alone. Always the guidance, the companionship, the love is there.

You may ask, 'But what of the depraved, the wrongdoer, the wicked, the cruel—are they being guided and cared for?' As White Eagle says, even those in spirit dare not judge the situation and condition of another soul and the forces which make him or her act as they do, so we certainly cannot judge them. But is not the need of the apparently 'lost' even greater than that of the soul who has seen the light? Still the guide is with them, but of course the response may be minimal, in which case the guide cannot come close. It is not easy for the guide to penetrate with his or her love the dense layers of earthiness imprisoning the soul; but when the soul, consciously or unconsciously, cries out for help, then the guide is there.

White Eagle wants us to add, 'Don't run away with the idea that guides are always of the male sex, for nothing could be further from the truth. The brotherhood of all time is perfectly balanced and the brethren come as man or woman according to the need of the soul in their care at a particular time. And when the time comes for the soul to pass on into the land of light, the guide is there to welcome that soul, all love … all love.'

How can one see and recognize one's guide or teacher in meditation?

There is a saying, 'When the pupil is ready, the master comes', and we think this is also very true of the guide of the spirit. At just the right moment, when you are ready and the knowledge will truly help you, then you will see and recognize your guide. You can prepare for this by talking to them in your heart, even if you cannot see them; in your quiet times or in meditation, just know that your guide is truly with you, and open yourself to receive their guidance and help. It may be that your first real awareness will come through your feeling a touch on your shoulder or on your head; or you may become aware of the warm handclasp of one who is leading you through the spirit garden, or into the temple, or by the waters of the still lake. But you have to do your part; you have to learn to be aware.

White Eagle teaches that the deep link with the guide of our spirit is through the higher self, to which, through our meditation, we shall become increasingly attuned. That growing attunement affects our outer lives too, and makes it easier for our guide to communicate with us.

I feel I have to add that when you have done the preparatory work, and are ready, it is quite possible that the full awareness of the personality and presence of your guide and of the name by which he or she wishes to be known may suddenly flash upon you, or be given you in a quite unexpected way (not necessarily during meditation); and you have to be alert in order to recognize it when it comes. You will need to learn too to recognize and interpret the pointers and symbolic pictures which may be their way of communicating with you.

Is there any difference between Mother Earth and Divine Mother?

Yes, there is a difference; and yet at the same time, the two are one. During the Piscean Age, from which humanity is now emerging, God, the infinite and eternal Spirit from whom all life came, has been thought of in relation to human kind as Father—the positive, masculine power or will ray of life. But White Eagle, following the Ancient Wisdom, describes the Great Spirit as being dual in nature, both Father and Mother—the heavenly Father, the first great Cause, the positive, outgoing aspect; and Divine Mother, the negative, receptive, conserver and preserver of all life. When we speak of Divine Mother we are thinking of that mother aspect of the Great Spirit; that aspect of God which nurtures and sustains and gives form to all life and beauty through the angels who work under her. We, her children, may feel her beautiful influence as an all-enfolding love and a sustaining wisdom. Sometimes we feel this influence almost like angels' wings around us, bringing a feeling of strength and comfort and steadiness. The angels of birth, into physical form, and of death, or withdrawal into form in the inner world—another kind of birth—work under her, as do the angels whose work is concerned with form in nature.

In meditation, we first aspire to the heart of the great Sun; we are just aware of light, of being in the light, in the heart of the great Sun if you like. All is light: there is no form, nothing except this great light. As Grace Cooke says:

> In meditation you are first made aware of the *reality* of light. This light is essentially the light of God, from which all subsequent vision and revelation and experience is born.... Out of light everything that has form was made.

from MEDITATION, pp. 25–26

And so, in our meditation, gradually the light begins to take form for us, the form of colour, symbols, sound—even the form of our guide and teacher or those whom we love in the land of light. Usually our first awareness of form in meditation is in the beauty of nature, perhaps in the natural form of the infinite and eternal garden: the trees, the flowers and the creatures of earth and air and water, and of the Sun. At the same time we may perceive the life-force behind and beneath all form.

It is the angels working under Divine Mother who help to make us aware of beauty in form; who, in meditation, work with us to create form. Thus Divine Mother gives form to all beauty, even as the earthly mother gives birth to the child, that little light from God, in human form. The beauty of the earth about us, the flowers, the trees, the everlasting hills and the whole of nature; the beauty and generosity of Mother Earth, which sustains our physical life; all such beauty is an expression, in form, of the love of Divine Mother for her children. So, although the two terms Divine Mother and Mother Earth have different meanings, they are not unconnected. The earth is a creation of Divine Mother; but the earth is not *just* matter: the earth herself has a spiritual being at her heart. Truly she is Mother Earth.

We could find so much comfort and strength in difficult times—particularly when, perhaps unconsciously, we are bearing the burden of another's need—if we could, in our hearts, give the problem or the person who is our concern into the care of Divine Mother. Her love is infinitely greater than anything we know or can ever comprehend. She can and does appear sometimes in form, at a certain level of consciousness, as a being of light, in a form so gracious, so serene, that to go towards her is almost like being enfolded in the wings of an angel. And yet at the same time we can sense from this gracious being a feeling of almost human warmth, as of a mother's love: comforting, healing and reassuring.

Many times in meditation we lift our hearts towards the great Sun and give ourselves into its golden light—the nearest our limited earthly minds can come to clothing the heavenly Father in form. We open our hearts to Christ the Son, the human form which comes to us from the heart of the great Sun; and from this communion we draw strength and light into our hearts. Yet we all—men and women, brother and sister alike—need also to attune ourselves often to this serene and lovely being, who is the personification in form, so far as we can conceive, of the Divine Mother of all life, who has all life in form in her care, and all that lives and breathes. We could be comforted and upheld in her love if we could think of her more often thus, and it would help us to give this love to others who are in special need of the mother's love and care—for instance, deprived, starving and abused children, as well as those who answer their need.

What a transformation there could be—and will be—in the consciousness of all human kind when the awareness of the mother aspect of the Great Spirit really awakens in all our hearts, so that she becomes a real, living being for us and we reflect her loving care for all life in form, through our lives!

The next question is on a subject closely allied to that of meditation, namely the power of prayer.

Can we really expect anything from prayer if our paths are already mapped out to lead us eventually to be man perfected? I find it difficult to sort out the difference between having to learn lessons, and 'paying' for past wrongdoings; and how much of these can be transmuted by prayer and listening to one's conscience and doing the best one can in each incarnation.

I do not think that there are many spiritual teachers who would encourage us to adopt so fatalistic an attitude of mind as to believe that everything is already mapped out for us, and that there is nothing that we can do to change it. The major events, yes: a certain karmic pattern of relationships to be healed or perfected, lessons to be learned, debts to be paid, opportunities for service. But we are faced with choices, small or great, from the moment we rise in the morning to the moment we lie down to sleep at night; and the choices we make determine the pattern of our future, certainly so far as the next life on earth is concerned, and to a great extent the pattern of this life as well. And although it may be true that we cannot alter the major events of our life, because they are predetermined by our karma, yet I do believe that there are occasions when a deep cry from the heart of the child of God can intervene to shape the course of events. Also, I believe that karma can be worked out at different levels and in different ways. Surely it is in the matter of everyday choices that true prayer comes in, so that we react in the very best way to everything that comes along?

True prayer is not to ask for this, that or the other, or that a problem be removed, or a circumstance altered. True prayer is an opening of the heart so that the sunlight of God's love and wisdom irradiates heart and mind and helps us to make the right choice. It helps us to resolve our karma so that instead of the pattern of life being tangled and painful, it becomes harmonious and creative. True prayer is to find the place in the still centre of our being, where the little flame of God burns, and to kneel before that flame. True prayer is to bow in total worship and surrender before God. True prayer is accepting in the spirit of thankfulness everything that comes. Then miracles happen, and karma is transmuted. There are many to testify to the truth of this. White Eagle tells us:

The truest and finest prayer is the one in which you ask nothing for yourself, only that you may know the love and the power and the wisdom of God. It is a yearning of the soul to be united with God. When a soul can pray like this, nothing on earth matters. It no longer cries out for this or that particular thing to happen, it does not seek its own gratification on any plane of life, it only seeks union with its creator. In this way every prayer is answered perfectly.

And on the subject of transmutation of karma White Eagle says,

If a soul, having his or her eyes opened to the saving power of love, and by the effort which that knowledge causes him or her to make, sends forth love, manifests love in his or her physical life, then the experiences which his karma has prepared for him become unnecessary, because he has learnt to receive and give the wisdom of his heart-mind in service. He has learnt the secret of life, and therefore it is not inevitable that he should suffer in the form which his karma appears to indicate. Always, always, karma can be transmuted by the redeeming power of love.

CHAPTER VII

Tree of Light

I

FOR MOST of us, concerned as we are with our daily affairs, the greatest problem in meditation is how to still the busy mind; how to withdraw from that busyness into the inner stillness, the still temple of our soul, and then, how to prevent the mind from intruding upon that stillness.

This is where controlled and disciplined breathing comes in, as I explained earlier. This is partly because, astrologically speaking, the air element is connected with the faculty of thought and the unfoldment and development of the mental vehicles. In meditation, as the breathing pattern is controlled, so the mind responds to this discipline, becoming quieter with every gentle inbreath and outbreath. Quiet breathing and a quiet mind are inextricably linked.

Another outcome of concentration by the earthly

mind on the rhythmic movement of the breath is that the higher, creative mind by contrast becomes freer to lead you into the inner world, the world of light. Thus a quiet and sustained breathing-in of 'the breath of God' and becoming filled with light will, of itself, lead you into a meditative state. There the mind in the heart can reveal to you the heavenly truths of the inner world.

The 'Tree of Light' is a breathing routine which is, in itself, almost a meditation; it can also prepare you for deeper meditation by its effect of calming and steadying the outer mind and lifting the heart to the Sun. It is therefore a healing and inspiring start to any day. It is also a good physical exercise, helping you to stand straight and tall and relaxed.

If possible it should be performed out of doors, with your feet resting on Mother Earth and head and heart turned towards the Sun. If this is not possible, at least try to make sure that you are standing before an open window, so that you can look out towards the light; or failing that, let it be somewhere where you can feel quiet and at peace, with plenty of space around you. Stand barefoot, if you can, with your feet square and firm upon the floor or upon the ground, just slightly apart to give you balance. The feeling of being like a strong, firmly-rooted tree will help you.

Stand for a few moments with your hands cupped

together before your heart centre in an attitude of prayer, and imagine, if you can, a soft pink rose cradled there in your heart, gently opening to the sunlight which is shining down into it. Stand like this for a few moments, breathing gently and looking deeply into that beautiful light, and feel the silence, the stillness, the peace. Everything that is of the earth is receding further and further from you as you concentrate on that centre of light, that flower which is in your heart.

Now, when you are ready, let your arms fall to your sides, and begin to inhale deeply. Trace a circle with your arms, stretching them wide, wide as they will go, reaching right out to the furthest circumference of the circle, and then up as high as you can, stretching towards the spiritual Sun which is shining above you. Picture 1 on p. 98 shows the arms raised in exaltation towards the sun: go right on with the movement until the hands meet over your head (picture 2). Concentrate very deeply from your heart (and not just with the outer mind), upon the glorious Sun, and the living, creative Word which is at the heart of it—until for one moment, you, the shining spirit, are totally at one with the heart of the Sun.

As you breathe out, with hands together gently draw the light and the blessing of the golden Sun right down through the centre of your body into your heart (picture 3); imagine this golden ray from the heart of the Sun pouring down and filling you with golden sunlight. Pause for a moment with your hands cupped at your heart centre, feeling, seeing, experiencing again that light glowing in the rose at the centre of your being. Then, as you gently bring your hands down by your sides to complete the movement, the light from the Sun passes right down through your body into Mother Earth, blessing her. It is as though the spirit and the flesh, heaven and earth, are becoming one.

Then start the cycle again, stretching your arms wide, reaching right out to the furthest circumference of the circle (think of it as a circle of light) as you breathe in. You may now feel an almost physical opening of your heart centre, as though you are making room for the light which you now draw down from the Sun, just as you did on the first breath. From that centre in your heart the light of the Sun reaches to every cell of your being, both physical and etheric, 'cleansing, healing, restoring, renewing'. That light in you, the Sun in you, gives light and health and strength to your whole body.

By the time you have drawn six or seven of these deep and life-giving breaths, I am sure you will feel strong and light-filled. Remember, though, that as well as the physical and etheric bodies you have just filled with light, you also have mental and emotional bodies, and that it can be helpful consciously to draw the light into these also.

First, the mental body. Following exactly the same physical routine, breathe in the light, and on the outbreath think of the light you are drawing down as the pure and lovely life-giving air element; the angel of the air is blessing you, and your mental body is being cleansed and filled with light and peace, is being made clear and vital and receptive to inspiration from the spirit.

Then it is the turn of the emotional body. As you draw the light down from that point in the heart of the Sun, it heals and brings peace to your emotional body, helping you to let go of all the little fears and resentments and tensions we normally hold. The emotional body is cleansed and illumined and at peace, and you, the real you, are in control, master in your own kingdom. The Sun is shining on the still waters of your soul.

Take as many breaths for each body (physical, etheric, mental, emotional) as you feel you need to, and then end with the hands in prayer over the heart centre, feeling again that you are enfolded in the radiant light that is glowing there, that you are at the heart of the rose. Pause for a moment or two, centred there in the stillness, feeling the quietness and radiance of the spirit. Now go on to the next stage of the routine, as follows:

As you breathe in, lift your hands (still together as in prayer) higher and higher up across the centre of your body, reaching towards the Sun. Feel that you are now drawing the light and strength from Mother Earth right up through your body—up through the trunk of the tree of golden light—and offering all that you are, your weakness and your strength, your fears and your thankfulness, into the heart of the Sun. Pause.... Then, as you breathe out, with palms facing downward, spread your arms again wide, as wide as you can, seeing them as branches of your tree of light or arms of a great cross of light (picture 4); do this with all the love in your heart you can, radiating the healing blessing of the Sun, the love of the Golden One, the Great Healer, to all humanity.

It is quite helpful to pause when your arms are level with your shoulders, and to turn the palms upward again towards the Sun. Then take another deep breath, lifting your arms a little towards the Sun again, with the feeling that you are opening your heart to the Sun's blessing; then, as you turn your palms back downward towards the earth again, breathing out, feel that that same healing blessing is shining into the heart of Mother Earth and all the natural world.

With the final breath of the routine, when you spread your arms wide, you will get the feeling that you are being surrounded by a circle of light; indeed, that you, the child of God, are enfolded in the peaceful, beautiful wings of your guardian angel. Wait quietly, your hands at your heart, for a little while, centred in the light. You are at the centre of the cross of light within the circle of light.

Now gently bring yourself back to awareness of the physical world around you, and peacefully go your way .

II

As you become familiar with this Tree of Light breathing, you may find yourself creating your own variations on the theme. That is to say, while the physical movement and the breath remains the same, the inner experience it inspires may change according to your need and your aspiration.

For instance, it is beautiful, particularly if you are out of doors, close to the earth and with the blue sky above you, to use it to help you commune with the angels. (You can stand in the rain with joy too, feeling the water angel's cleansing blessing and her refreshment to your spirit!) Unlike us—heavy and earthbound—the angels are free from the burden of incarnation; they serve God's purposes as the perfect embodiment of a quality or element of being. Thus they are all life and joy and light, and all love too—

perfect manifestations of aspects of the Godhead. Humanity has lived so long in isolation, unaware of the angelic lifestream, but in the new age the 'true brotherhood of angels and men', as it is described, humanity and the angels working together in harmony, will become a living reality. And as we learn to know them and to love and serve with them, so we too shall be filled with light, and the burden of flesh—incarnation—will be lifted.

As a way to establish this contact with the angels, let us use our beautiful Tree of Light to help us, so that not only as we consciously breathe but at all times we can open our hearts to them and their influence, and be thankful to them. Don't worry if you can't actually see them. The angelic form is not easy to see; angels are all colour and light, moving in harmony, though they can also be very still and strong. Just try to feel them, to be with them, to be enfolded in their light and quality of consciousness.

Stand firm and steady on Mother Earth, and as you breathe, aspiring towards the Sun, think of the angelic hosts who come from the Sun almost as streams of light and colour and pure feeling, and yet with form and consciousness. Some of them serve a great purpose in the cosmos, others are more deeply concerned with the life and consciousness of human kind. You will find, if you do this, that you will for a time be lifted right out of the heaviness of earth into a world of light and colour and harmony.

Try, then, to particularize—that is to say, according to the need you feel and the mood of the day, from your heart invoke a particular angel, trying to become absorbed into the light and colour and above all the quality of consciousness of that angelic being. Not only for yourself is the help invoked, for as you become attuned you also become a channel, and the outbreathing of blessing upon humanity radiates the particular quality that angel being represents. This contact can either be made while actually performing the breathing exercise, or as you stand erect, hands cupped before the heart, or fingertips together as in prayer, in the pause between the two stages of the complete exercise.

These are the angels, or angelic lifestreams, with whom communion seems to me to be specially valuable:

The Angel of Joy

Angels are not really either male or female, yet I always feel that the Angel of Joy is 'she'. She comes as a cleansing stream of sparkling water reflecting diamond or rainbow light, cleansing all heaviness from the aura—manifesting a dancing joy and a deep thankfulness to God.

The Angel of Peace

The Angel of Peace is so quiet and still and powerful, but she is all love. To me her garment is the softest blue like the sky, with a touch of rose pink and sunshine. It could almost be likened to mother-of-pearl. As you breathe in her influence, all care falls away, and your heart is stilled and stayed on God. As you breathe her influence out into the world, turbulent emotions are stilled: a quietness comes into the hearts of humanity.

The Angels of the Sun

They are glorious, all golden fire. They sweep through the consciousness with creative energy. They awaken sleeping humanity, dispelling all darkness. They come from the heart of the Sun in majesty. Tune in to the Angels of the Sun if you are feeling a bit feeble and low—they will fill you with strength and energy!

The Angels of the Home

These angels are beautiful to contemplate and by their very nature come close to the heart. Every home has its angel, but mostly we are oblivious to them, we shut them out. When we know how to invoke them we will bring harmony into the home, as they harmonize the disparate elements there and enfold us in a mantle of peace and love.

Feel peace descending into your home as you breathe in the angels' blessing, and as you breathe out try to feel their gentle influence blessing the homes of men and women all over the world.

The Angel of Life

You might call this the Angel of the Earth Mother. She takes you into the kingdom of nature, of growing things. She is gentle and tender, but immutable. To me, she is in shining white raiment with, somewhere in the light, a soft and heavenly green. As you breathe in, contemplating the Angel of Life, you become caught up in the life which flows in tree and flower, and which springs from the earth in constant renewal—all things made new by the Angel of Life. When there is devastation on earth, the angel brings into being new life to heal the scars and bring new beauty. As in nature, so this regeneration takes place in the human form too.

Then there are of course *the Angels of the Elements,* that is, the angels of the Earth, Air, Fire and Water. As you contemplate these great beings, giving yourself, in your mind, into the element they represent, you will have your own revelation of their work with humanity. So also with the great angel beings representing the triune aspects of God, *the Angel of Wisdom, the Angel of Love,* and *the Angel of Power.*

These are but a few of those who come so close to human kind seeking an awakening consciousness of their presence. We need to be still and 'self-less', and have a loving heart. Then we shall know them.

III

Another variation on the Tree of Light which can be very helpful is to use the breath in conjunction with the Lord's Prayer. This then becomes a very beautiful brief meditation, spoken phrase by phrase.

So: stand really tall, shoulders dropped, heart opening to the Sun; breathe gently for a second or two, becoming centred in your heart, and your hands together in the prayer position before your heart.

Now, drop your hands to the side and begin the routine. *Our Father which art in heaven*—say the words silently in your heart as you breathe in, stretching the arms wide, as far as they can go, and then up, up, reaching right up into the Sun, into the heavens. Really feel that you are reaching up into the heart of the Sun.

Hallowed be Thy Name—then gently breathe out, bringing your hands down the centre of your body, in the prayer position, to rest upon your heart. Hallowed, holy, be Thy Name.... The creative Word, the creative power of God is in my heart. Holy ... holy ... holy....

Thy kingdom come—stretch wide again, as wide as you can, as you breathe in the holy breath, lifting your arms right up into the Sun once more. Thy kingdom come in me.... Say the words in your heart and have the feeling of total surrender of all that you are into that great light; total surrender to the will of God.

Thy will be done on earth as it is in heaven—draw the hands down again through the centre of the body to rest upon the heart in an attitude of prayer, so drawing the light of the great Sun into your heart. Thy will be done on earth, in me, in all levels of my being.... May the Sun shine from my heart as it shines in the heavens.... The feeling again is of surrender—Thy way, not mine O Lord. *Thy* way....

Give us this day our daily bread—again spread the arms wide as you breathe in, and see with the vision of your heart (or in your imagination) fields of waving corn, and give thanks to God, the Mother of us all, for the fruits of the earth which feed us. As you breathe out, once again bringing the hands down through the centre of the body, accept with thankfulness all the experiences of each day through which the soul is nourished. Accept them thankfully and pray that you may use them wisely: they are the daily bread of the spirit.

Forgive us our trespasses—take another deep, full breath, spreading the arms wide and reaching up into the healing light of the Sun, feeling the love of the Great Healer pouring down into your heart, cleansing, healing, forgiving.... *As we forgive those who trespass against us.* As you breathe out, again draw that cleansing, healing light right down into the rose of your heart.... May the light of the Sun and the love of the Great Healer cleanse and heal you and help you let go of any pain or hurt. May it shine from the rose in your heart in love and understanding and forgiveness.

And lead us not into temptation—now as you breathe in, spread wide in surrender, reaching up to the Sun; and as you do so, feel that you are surrounded, held safe, in a circle of protective light.... *But deliver us from evil*—as you breathe out, bring your hands down the centre of your body, drawing the light right down into your heart, cleansing, healing, making perfect.... Deliver us from all evil. You will find that your movements have created a cross of light in the centre of the circle. You are held safe, secure in the heart of that ancient symbol of the cross of light within the circle of light.

For Thine is the kingdom, the power and the glory—again as you breathe in, you have that feeling of total surrender, of giving yourself utterly into the Sun. Pause if you can, at the peak of your breath, as your hands are reaching up into the Sun, to savour for a moment that wonderful feeling of being totally absorbed into the Sun. *For ever and ever, amen*—as you breathe out, bring your hands down to your heart centre, to rest upon your heart. Amen. *Aum.... Aum.... Aum....*

*

You may feel now that you just want to sit down and continue your meditation, resting in that still centre of power within yourself. Then, when you are ready, bring yourself gently back, seal yourself as I have already described, and return to your earthly business.

If you don't want to continue the meditation, just stand for a moment or two, consciously at the centre of the cross of light within the protective circle of light, and then go your way with thankfulness.

CHAPTER VIII

'Abounding blessing': a teaching by White Eagle

EVERY SOUL living on earth is in a physical body in order to build and create in due time that body of light which the ancient brotherhoods called the solar body. The power which commands the light and creates man's solar body is the power of love.

When you are blessed with the gift of clear vision, or clairvoyance, you will be able to see the solar body of your brother just above his physical form. Within or above every man and woman (and child too, if they have reached a certain level) is to be seen this beautiful solar body, or body of light, created out of the light of the Son, the Christos.

We are not speaking of an orthodox individual person. We are speaking of the Son of the Father–Mother God, the pure White Light which is in the Sun and which descends to the earth from its Creator. Think about our words, because there is a deeper truth here than may at first appear. The Son of God is the heavenly light of the Sun; and every living thing is permeated with the Sun and with the light.

Now we will leave this theme for a moment, because we want to touch on the power of thought. We do this because thought has such a great part to play, not only in man's spiritual evolution, but in the evolution of what we shall call the etheric life, for by your thought you can mould the ether as you will. Very often this is an unconscious moulding, but when men and women develop better understanding and realize that their *own thought* is moulding etheric matter into form, they will naturally want to discipline their thinking so that they create beauty, goodness and harmony. The form thought creates depends on the degree of love, or light, in the individual man or woman.

The whole purpose of the Brotherhood of the Great White Light is to help men and women to develop and discipline their minds towards good, happy, kind and beautiful thought. Did not St Paul say, *Whatsoever things are true, whatsoever things are honest, whatsoever things are just, whatsoever things are pure, whatsoever things are lovely, whatsoever things are of good report ... think on these things?** Paul knew that a brother must train himself to use

*Philippians 4 : 8

this wonderful gift of thought-power in the right way.

Now the Master Jesus, through many incarnations, prepared and developed the perfect solar body or body of light through which Christ, the Son, was able to manifest; for when the body of light has been created in man, the whole physical body becomes illumined, and a purer vehicle for the use of the soul.

We are endeavouring to help you in your meditations by the power of God-thought to develop this solar body, this body of the Sun: for meditation (and through meditation finding the creative centre of love and light within the innermost being) is the only way in which the soul can consciously develop that pure body of light. This is why meditation was practised in the mystery schools and the brotherhoods of the past, and why the brethren withdrew from the material life into communities or brotherhoods, dwelling in high places, raised above worldliness.

In your meditation you are told first of all to rise into the heights, because by so doing you are withdrawing from the clamour of the thought-forms and all the mists which gather around you at the material level of life. So in the meditation class, first of all our teachers take us right up into the heights, to the golden apex of the mountain, where we become absorbed in a glorious heavenly light. At this moment we touch the true light, and begin to create and develop a solar body. If you do nothing else during your meditation but become enabled for a few moments to bask in that pure and true light, you are still doing very well. Later on, you will be told to use your higher mind to create a picture, to create form, at that inner level.

We want you to understand that the divine mind in you can manipulate the higher ether, the white ether, to create beautiful and perfect form. People who do not understand will think this is all imagination, and that nothing created in this way is real; but the ether is a very real substance, more real than physical matter, and the higher or divine mind in you can mould that sensitive ether into living form. If, for instance, in your meditations you can enter the healing temple and see the healing angels at work, you are helping in the creation of life itself at that higher level. What you see is true and real because it is created by the power of God in you and with the help of heavenly beings.

You notice great changes on earth. Remarkable inventions are coming as the result of great mental activity; but there is always a tendency through man's own weakness and lack of discipline, for such mental activity to become destructive. This humanity has to watch, especially at the present time, because this stimulation and growth of the mental body of mankind could so easily prove destructive. We are trying to show you a clear picture.

On the one side see the creative power used for good; think of the countless numbers of people who are now inwardly urged to do good; think of all the groups and societies working for the good of mankind; see the efforts of the young people with good and creative impulses who want to abolish all that is holding back human development and the wellbeing of mankind. Then, on the other hand, there is the array of dark, destructive thought which finds entry into highly developed minds to create instruments of destruction, as well as to stimulate destructive passions and emotions.

We in the Brotherhood are working to bring harmony and balance in human life. We tell you this so that you too may work in your own way; so that you will discipline yourself to think and create forms of goodness, beauty and harmony; and at the same time dismiss all dark, destructive, antagonistic thoughts; all thoughts of sickness and despair.

The old philosophers used to say, 'as above, so below'. As you see in your meditations, as you learn to meditate wisely, truly, so you will bring through into manifestation on earth that which you see shining above, in that state of meditation. Remember, dear brethren and friends, that you are God's instruments on earth. Life is good! Live to glorify your Creator! To give light, to give love, to heal through good, loving, positive thought of good, of God. This is the work of every true brother of the light.

CHAPTER IX

A teaching : 'The divine magic'

WE HAVE spoken to you on a number of occasions about the white magic, and of how the secret of all the mystery schools was the knowledge of how to use this magical power which lies dormant in all people. So-called miracles are demonstrations of this white magic; although we must add that no initiate will waste time and power to satisfy the curious. Demonstrations of this magic are only given to bless, to uphold, and to help souls realize their divine potentialities.

In the mystery schools of old it was taught that no soul could rush forward into the temple. Indeed, the very nature of the spiritual unfoldment necessary before the soul can enter into the holy temple makes this impossible. Sometimes it seems a very long journey up the mountain, and souls get weary and discouraged and think that they will never reach their goal. We understand the weariness of the flesh and the mind and the spirit, but we know also that without fail a sustaining, refreshing grace comes, which upholds the weary traveller on his or her journey.

Knowledge purely as a mental attainment is of little use to the soul as it seeks entrance into the mysteries. This is why we encourage you to devote time to meditation and contemplation.

Now some think that meditation means to sit still thinking beautiful thoughts, but that in itself will not get you very far. Correct meditation releases the soul from the bondage of the physical senses and enables it to rise through the various planes of life right up to the peak at which illumination comes; and when illumination comes it brings with it knowledge. The soul practised in meditation learns to approach the temples of wisdom, and there, in the silence, receives from the teachers the knowledge and the understanding of spiritual law which it seeks. Some are able to rise only to a limited height; they see writing, they see symbols, or characters in a language they do not understand. The symbols, the characters mean nothing until the soul has the key which will enable it to interpret the symbols.

Now, the pupil in the mystery schools is taught that the key to understanding of these symbols is in the golden chamber; and the golden chamber is the heart, called by some the golden lotus; and within this golden flower lies the key which will unlock the door of the mysteries. You can read many books. You can accumulate many facts. You can go through ceremonies. You can witness or take part in wonderful rituals which will stir your emotional body, or even stimulate the higher mind to a degree—but none of these will of themselves give you the power to enter the temple and understand the secrets of the inner mysteries.

Everything needed by the aspirant for his entry into the Great White Lodge lies within himself. No school on the outer plane can give you this knowledge. The only school in which you will gain this precious wisdom is the school of life; you will learn through human life and experience and human relationships on the outer plane, and through meditation on the inner plane. The outer action and the inward contemplation and meditation must go hand in hand if the aspirant is to find the lost secret, the divine magic.

The secret in meditation is to get beneath all thought. Do not think your way through meditation. You must go beneath the surface of thought to the point of stillness, deep within. This we call the 'dot within the circle': the symbol of the Sun, the central point from which no master can err.

In the mystery schools every candidate is led eventually to a chapel or a cell which has no furnishings but a mirror, and has to be ready and strong enough to look into the mirror and see the true reflection of him or herself. To the one who is truly searching this can be a moment of divine illumination. It is a moment of initiation when everything extraneous is shed, and the soul rises and becomes united with the source of its being.

Now you may begin to see why meditation and outward living must go hand in hand, because in meditation the soul becomes aware of truth, and the life lived must be a demonstration of the truth revealed in meditation.

Heaven is a state of supreme happiness and joy, reached when the soul comprehends the power of the divine magic. Yet this magic is so elusive, and cannot be put into words; it is a divine essence with which the soul is filled, almost unconsciously. A master is natural, is all love, is gentle. A master dominates no-one but loves all: thus does he or she demonstrate the divine magic, and the divine magic is a power which will remove every obstacle, overcome all difficulties, make crooked places straight. It will bring peace in place of storm. The Master Jesus demonstrated that when he rose in the boat and stilled the waves. The boat is a symbol of the soul. His very presence—the divine presence, the divine magic—overcame the storm of emotion.

Do you see the reason why karma is a barrier? Karma, my children, is really unlearned lessons. These lessons have to be faced in a calm spirit. Rejoice in your karma. Thank God for the opportunities which are presented to you to learn lessons and dispose of your karma, for these are steps by which you mount into the Great White Lodge above. Every piece of karma gone through means a lesson learned, but the most important thing for you to remember is, do not just try to get past your karma; be sure you have learned the lesson which the episode was intended to teach. If you have not learned the lesson and have just skirted round your karma, you have only put it on the shelf and it will come back again and again until the lesson has been learned.

Is this hard? But it is true, and we are trying to show you and to help you, because we love you. We are your brethren. We have passed your way. We have ways to travel beyond and beyond and beyond the earth, but when we look upon karma, the obstacle lessons which are placed before us, we accept them with thanksgiving. This is why we say on many occasions, accept, accept, accept the conditions in your life and be thankful for them, for they are steps leading to illumination and perfect happiness.

The secret of the divine magic comes to you when you have overcome, when you have learnt to master the lower self and to manifest divine love, gentleness, kindness: when you have learnt not to retaliate or be resentful. The initiate resigns all injustice, however great or small, to divine law. He knows that the oil-press of the law crushes the olives, and the oil of wisdom remains. The hardships, the inequalities, the difficulties, the injustices of life are all ground in the press of God, and the pure oil of wisdom, the pure wine of life, remains.

The wise man or woman will not seek to justify himself or herself, but resigns all in perfect confidence and faith to the exact outworking of the law of God, of love.

Now, peace, true lasting peace be with you. Remember the gentle way, the gentle answer, the relinquishing of all demands. Thy will, not my will, be done, O God.

Children, the Master is present. Open your hearts and receive His blessing. He stands in your midst, the perfect Son of God. We bow before Him.

CHAPTER X

A teaching:
'Beside the still waters'

WE WANT to say something to you about true religion. True religion is not tied to any creed or dogma, it is not merely some form of belief. Religion is the growing consciousness of God in man's own being. When man becomes awakened to the light of God, the Christ within him, the Son of God, starts to grow; and this growing God-consciousness is his strength and stay, his comfort and his guide. This is true religion, and it is what all humanity is searching for.

Today, western man has to a large extent foregone organized religion, but he is still seeking for God in many ways; but he will not get very far until he learns that the God he seeks is in himself. He can learn about this infinite, this vital truth only through the love which he can feel for others, and the compassion for the sufferings, the inharmony and pain which shadow his brother's life. When he recognizes these he starts to think what he can do to alleviate this suffering, and then the first glimmerings of religion dawn in man's heart. Thereafter he will desire to change his own life, wanting to live in accordance with his new inner feeling—a feeling of love, of love for God growing slowly in his heart. As this feeling of concern and love for his brother grows, it enfolds more than human life; it expands into other worlds, into the animal, the natural kingdoms; then beyond all physical form into the etheric and so into the mental kingdom and to the celestial kingdom. The consciousness of God, which once started as a tiny spark, grows and expands until finally that soul embraces all life, both physical and spiritual; there is no limitation to his consciousness of God. Then this man can no longer harm his brother by thought or word or deed. He becomes gentle in his ways, meek but never weak. Remember the example of Jesus—not only his gentle nature, his meekness, but also his resolute strength, his moral courage, and his unfailing pity for those who sinned and suffered.

Humanity, in its search for religion, must look beyond the shells of orthodoxy, creed and dogma, for the indwelling spirit in its brother man. True religion in a man or woman give them complete conviction, beyond shadow of doubt, that they cannot die and that those whom they love can never die. They need no proof of continuing life after death. They already know, because the light within them reveals higher worlds of a purer ether into which the spirit passes.

If you will read the twenty-third psalm, you will find there a light to lead you to true religion. Say to yourselves daily: *The Lord is my shepherd; I shall not want....* The Lord is the power within you. The Lord also enfolds you, feeds and clothes you, and gives you a place in which to live. True, you also have to make some effort of your own, but this is really the God within you making the effort, did you but understand. Man only lives by reason of this impetus from the God within him. Without this continued impetus, he would die. Man has to work to supply his daily needs. Nevertheless, it is the God within who is his shepherd, guiding, succouring, lifting him up when he falls down. *The Lord is my shepherd, I shall not want; he maketh me to lie down in green pastures; he leadeth me beside still waters.* How many of you know the meaning of the 'still waters'? They are that state of consciousness when you quietly wait upon God in prayer and meditation; and here beside the still waters you see the light, and receive inspiration; you are raised in consciousness through your contemplation and meditation by the still waters.

He restoreth my soul. When you make your contact with God in the silence, you are restored in soul—

restored by the blessed, glorious and universal Father and Mother God. You are lifted up, given strength; you see the light and you know that in future you must work not only for yourself, but for all this life of spirit of which you are dimly becoming aware. You know that if you fall down, or if you sin by wrong thought, wrong words, wrong actions, you will suffer as well as making others suffer, becoming a drag on the wheels of spiritual progress.

Think! By your thoughts and particularly your words—for the foolish word so lightly spoken can wound very deeply—you create sorrow and sickness and trouble for others. My brethren, if you would be servers of the human race it is important that you guard your tongues so that you shed no darkness into the lily of an expanding religion which is filling the hearts of many souls. We see so often from the spirit life heedless tongues doing much harm. The man or woman of God has to learn to think rightly and to speak rightly, which means to think and speak lovingly and kindly and truly. Did not Jesus say that it is better that a millstone be tied round a man's neck and he be flung into the sea than that he should destroy the faith of one of these little ones?

The power of thought is the greatest power of life. Yet when we look upon the earth, even in good places, we see oh! such a dark mass of tangled weeds where there could be beautiful flowers growing in lovely gardens.

How then can spiritual servers of religion help humanity to find their God within them? By the power of thought, God-thought. Through many lives we who speak have written and spoken on this one theme of the power of man's thought, and how to broadcast the light of God. But it is difficult; and all who take this task upon themselves must strictly discipline themselves as to what they think and what they say.

Do not be despondent. We are not saying that young children can do what adults can (we mean children and adults in spiritual growth). The motive to broadcast God's will, God's word, must be there in the heart. We were once asked what effect one man's good, positive and constant thought would exert on humanity. In answer we reminded you of the cities Sodom and Gomorrah. The Lord, so your bible tells you, said that if there were only a few men in those cities who were true God-men, the cities could be saved. Yet those few were still lacking and the cities were destroyed.

We say to you most earnestly that if a small group of people such as gather in this Lodge could be constant and positive in their God-thought and in their love to their fellows in daily life, the whole earth could be caught up in the light and power of the Creator. The power of the Creator works through every atom of this planet. You are such atoms. The object of life here is for spirit to illumine dark, dense matter and raise it to a much finer ether; and by your God-thought you are helping to accomplish this work. Planets and worlds exist all around you which are out of range of this earth; they are in the light. Presently scientists will discover that the universe is not wholly physical matter*; they will begin to help people to find the God-consciousness within themselves. When this day comes there will be no death, no destruction on earth, because it will have passed onward from the vibration of destruction and disaster; it will have reached a higher etheric state.

Remember that although you appear to be lonely you do not work alone. Angels and elder brethren and companions of the spirit are with you, watching over you, my children. The angels know you and all that you do; they therefore pour forth their compassion, devoting time and love to healing you physically, mentally, and in your soul.

The world today needs all the positive God-thought that you can project, not only to heal the sick in body but the sick in mind. We suggest that

*These words were of course given well before physical scientists developed their current view of matter.

each one of you in the silence of your own soul will kneel beside the still waters and pray to be able to send forth the healing light of the Son of God, the Christ. If you cannot do it every minute of your day, then send it forth at the magical hour of noon. Project light to the whole earth, to all suffering humanity. Behind you is a power beyond your comprehension; It only waits for its children to be willing to be channels. It only waits for you to serve, knowing that you are nothing. May the channel open wide and the light flood through! By your mental direction it can go forth to heal the nations, to heal the whole world and to raise it from death and darkness into everlasting light and glory. So mote it be!

A FINAL WORD FROM OUR
GENTLE BROTHER OF THE SPIRIT

MY DEAR ones, enter the silence often. Be still at least for a short time every day, morning and night. Surely God is worthy of a little attention in your busy life? Whenever you can, withdraw from the crowd, seek contact with that divine Life, which you will recognize in yourself as a vibration or feeling of peace, of love, and of great light. You can carry that light in your heart as you go amid the crowds.

In your meditation, think often of the beauty of God, the love of God; and as you do so you will begin to feel within your heart a pulsation of love, divine peace and kindness towards the whole world, and see God manifesting in all life, in all form. Those who thus 'practise the presence of God' can enter a crowd, or a room full of people, and consciously or unconsciously they are radiating light, they are projecting the light of the divine spirit. This is the healing light, the light of the world. Christ, through Jesus, said, *I am the light of the world.* I AM. The Christ in you is the light of your world and the light of mankind.

Seek the will of God, and not self-will.... Go into the silence; seek there, and then when you have found it, let it manifest in your own lives. Put aside all temptation to harbour unkind or critical words or thoughts. In their place let there be consideration and thoughtfulness, remembering the difficulties that all, including yourselves, have to encounter. This is the law of Christ, and this is what Christ did through his servant Jesus of Nazareth. Go ye and do likewise and you will have nothing to fear. Instead you will unfurl your wings and rise into the world of great joy, light and peace.

God bless you all. Be comforted; and set about putting your life on these true lines, which will lead you directly to the kingdom of heaven. God bless you, every one.